The Toltec Tarot

Heather Ash Amara
Illustrations by Indigo Flores

Toltec Center of Creative Intent

Toltec Center of Creative Intent
www.tolteccenter.org
512 233 8480

Copyright 2006. All rights reserved. No parts of this book may be reproduced or transmitted in any form or by any means, electronic or mechanical, including photocopying, recording, or by an informational storage and retrieval system, or other without written permission of the publisher.

Second Edition Spring 2009

Contents

Introduction..........5
How To Use the Toltec Tarot..........11
Toltec Tarot Mythology..........19
Fool..........29
Magician..........35
High Priestess..........41
Empress..........47
Emperor..........53
Hierophant..........59
Lovers..........65
Chariot..........71
Strength..........77
Hermit..........83
Wheel of Fortune..........89
Justice..........95
Hanged One..........101
Death..........107
Temperance..........113
Devil..........119
Tower..........125
Star..........131
Moon..........137
Sun..........143
Judgment..........149
Cosmos..........155
Acknowledgments..........161
Resources..........163

INTRODUCTION

While the first printed form of the Tarot appeared in Italy in the 1400's, speculation continues that the Tarot pictures may have been created in Egypt, China, or perhaps have originated in Jewish Kabalah as sacred teaching templates. Despite the uncertainty surrounding its beginnings, the Tarot has survived through the centuries to become a beloved friend and inspiration in modern times.

Whatever the Tarot's foundation, in the past twenty years it has blossomed in a variety of forms, growing from the roots of a few well-known decks (such as the Rider-Waite and Builders of the Adytum Tarot) into varied individualized and riveting forms. From the round, women-centered and multi-cultural MotherPeace Tarot to the visionary, collage Voyager deck, from Celtic to Native American to African Tarot decks, from the Catwomen Tarot to the Transcendental Zen cards — the abundance of choices is remarkable!

Into this garden of artistic and spiritual creativity, we are grateful to offer a unique hybrid blossom, grown from the fertile soil of shamanic wisdom and Toltec teachings.

I was introduced to the Tarot through Vicki Noble, co-creator of the MotherPeace deck. In 1978, one year after encountering their first Tarot deck, Vicki and Karen Vogel spontaneously began to envision a new Tarot, based in the wisdom of ancient Goddess-worshipping cultures. These revolutionary cards inspired me to begin my journey of healing using the Tarot images as allies and "sacred play" and led to an intensive shamanic healing program through the MotherPeace Institute. I was then blessed to continue my Tarot studies with Cerridwen Fallingstar who taught me new ways of opening to Tarot symbolism and was instrumental in moving me from a Tarot dabbler to a committed student.

In 1994, I met don Miguel Ruiz, author of *The Four Agreements*. Walking through a parking lot on the way to dinner, I told him, "I want to apprentice with you and learn the Tarot." He grabbed the hat off my head, put it on his own, and giggled. And thus, I began a six-year apprenticeship with don Miguel, from whom I learned much more than the Tarot. I learned how to completely recreate my life from the inside out.

I was inspired to approach don Miguel after he shared his story of meeting the Tarot. One day during his weekly dreaming session with his mother Sarita, don Miguel found himself standing facing rows of pictures in a small stone vault. All of his usual techniques for waking up from a vision did not work, and he panicked after realizing that he could not leave. Breathing through his fear, he understood that he must dream into the pictures before he could leave. As he performed this task, the meaning of each image flooded his being. "I was so excited," he later related, "that I could not understand the images any more. I had to find stillness again before they would reveal themselves to me."

When don Miguel returned from his dream, he searched

Introduction

for a Tarot deck that resembled the images that he had seen. The closest images were from the Rider-Waite deck.

For the first years of my apprenticeship with don Miguel, I immersed myself in the more traditional Rider-Waite Tarot and in the foundations of Toltec shamanism. I slowly gathered other Tarot decks, playing with their similarities and differences. I read everything I could about Tarot, offered public Tarot readings, and taught Tarot 101 workshops at the University of California in Davis. During this time, I also traveled extensively with don Miguel to Teotihuacán, Mexico where I helped to assist and lead spiritual journeys. Toltec and Tarot thus continued to merge and blend in my conscious mind and subconscious being.

Amber Jayanti's book, *Living the Tarot*, propelled me beyond the two-dimensional images and into three-dimensional exploration. Why just look at the cards? Why not actually learn to BE them? And so I journeyed beyond thinking about Fool energy by actually becoming the joyful Fool. I embodied the deep stillness of the High Priestess. I danced with transformative Temperance. I hung upside down from trees, breathing in the willing Hanged One.

And as I embodied these archetypes, I noticed that I became fuller, more fearless, and increasingly willing to take risks. I could call on the timeless tools of my many new allies: the smile of the Strength card, the blade of Death, and the grace of the Star. My habitual patterns began to fall away. I did not have to act a particular way or hold to one particular identity. I began to see the Tarot not simply as a way to connect with intuition, but also as a path towards greater choice and freedom.

Fueled by my deepening realization of the power of the Tarot, I gathered all I had learned and wove it into an apprenticeship program that I created through the Toltec Center of Creative Intent. I saw Toltec and Tarot as great partners in supporting people to break apart old structures and limitations while embracing choice and freedom. And so in 2001, the SpiritWeavers program was born as a six-month shamanic apprenticeship program with a Toltec heart and a Tarot spine. To bridge the intensive monthly weekend gatherings, the groups meet weekly to learn to dream into the Tarot, focusing on one card per week. SpiritWeavers granted me five years to coalesce how best to share the marriage of Toltec and Tarot. During this time, I also authored my first book, *The Four Elements of Change*.

From the SpiritWeavers program came the two beings most instrumental in the birth of this new cross-cultural Toltec-Tarot being — Raven Smith and Indigo Flores. Raven was a bored systems administrator in Mountain View, CA who found the Toltec Center by doing a web-search for "Toltec" and "Tarot," two of his favorite tools. Over the years Raven became a dear friend, a SpiritWeavers teacher, a business partner, and then my beloved life mate. So I trusted Raven's instincts and guidance when he said, "The time has come for you to write your Tarot book." The creation of this book was further seeded when he invited Indigo to draw the cards' mystical images.

Introduction

Indigo is a marvelous elf, a magical being of mischief and twinkle. As a SpiritWeavers teacher, he blessed the Toltec Center with a large, colorful mural of the many sacred sites that we visited over the years. His ability to fluidly dream combined with his expressive lines and sensitivity to detail equipped him to be the perfect "father" of this creation. For six months, we sent draft writings and preliminary sketches back and forth over the Internet between California and Texas. We had no definitive vision of the end result, simply a trust that we would be guided, with Raven's assistance as a diligent butt-kicker to keep us both on task.

This Toltec Tarot child was birthed at the heart of Toltec wisdom in Teotihuacán. At our yearly pilgrimage to this fabled power center, we unveiled the final versions of the cards and the poems that accompany them. In the place where the Masters lived in Teotihuacán, we laid the Toltec Tarot cards out together for the first time and blessed the images. Now we offer them to you, so they may connect you to the ancient wisdom of the Tarot, the Toltec, and the magic of the sacred Toltec site named Teotihuacán, which translates as "the place where humans become God."

May these words and images guide you to reclaim both your humanity and your divinity, and may you dream yourself whole.

Heather Ash Amara
Teotihuacán, Mexico
July 2006

HOW TO USE THE TOLTEC TAROT

Arcana is the pluralized form of the Latin word arcanum, which means "deep secret or mystery." The major arcana are the heart of the Tarot, depicting twenty-two archetypical energies that are the keys to unlocking the secrets and mystery that reside in all of us. While the Tarot images have been linked most often with divination, they encompass much more than a method for reading the future. They are tools for opening the gates of our inner wisdom.

The Toltec are masters of the art of perception who are called "Artists of the Spirit." They lived over 2,000 years ago in Central Mexico, and today a growing number of people are using Toltec wisdom to reclaim their freedom and joy. Millions of people have tapped into Toltec teachings through the books of Carlos Castaneda, don Miguel Ruiz, and many other Toltec authors.

The Toltec path teaches that each of us has the capacity to create our own reality. Through our social conditioning at an early age, we learn to close ourselves down and to seek acceptance outside of ourselves. We take on many agreements and beliefs that limit our perceptions and lock us into a confining image of who we think we should be. Breaking free from this self-created image and reclaiming our essence is the goal of Toltec.

The Toltec Tarot is an easily accessible, highly effective addition to the toolbox of all spiritual and healing seekers.

All of us yearn to change our lives and move beyond habits and old emotions. Yet when we are in the midst of working, raising or maintaining a family, attending school, or living in general, it is often difficult to see how our actions create our reality. Few role models are available for making deep lasting changes that effectively convey us past our restrictive sense of safety.

OPENING THE GATES

The Tarot is a vast information source that can help us to delve into new ways of being, to re-establish internal balance, and to ignite inspiration. As you tap into each card energetically, it will open gateways within your being and usher new choices and fluidity into your life.

Each Toltec Tarot card vibrates at a frequency associated with its archetypal image. Archetypes are energetic patterns that are recognized as templates of human experiences and personalities. When we speak of "a fool" we understand each other by accessing the fool resonance.

Studying and dreaming into each of the Toltec Tarot cards allows us to explore those archetypes that we actively express in the world. With reflection, this aids us in restoring internal balance. The Toltec Tarot also introduces a plethora of role models that support us in making healthy changes in our habits, thoughts, and actions.

By embodying each of the Tarot cards, we become familiar with their unique vibration, and we gift our being with twenty-two different ways to react to any given situation. Instead of remaining fixated in a single habitual reaction, we can pause, feel through the Tarot frequencies, choose an appropriate one to work with, and then respond from a different point of perception. This breaks apart old stagnant structures and brings creativity and flexibility to our decision-making process. We broaden and deepen our understanding of how we get stuck and are able to select from a variety of means to set ourselves free.

To move beyond thinking about the cards and merely using them as an intellectual exercise, we must "dream" the cards into our life. Dreaming is the process of employing all of our senses and our imagination to experience something with our full being, not just our mind.

DREAMING THE TAROT

To build a new foundation for dreaming the Tarot, choose one card to work on at a time. I recommend starting with the Fool and sequentially moving through each card, so you can imprint the energy of each onto your being. Set a time frame to work with each card. We focus on one card a week in the SpiritWeavers program, although you may want to explore one card a day. Whatever you choose, you will reap the greatest benefit if you commit to a time frame and stay consistent. Once you have savored the initial flavor of each card, you can deepen your experience in a variety of ways.

The Toltec Tarot

((Visit http://www.toltectarot.com for more exercises with the Toltec Tarot and for specific practices for each card.)

Sit quietly with the image before you read anything about the card. First, close your eyes and center yourself. Using your breath, let go of any busyness or tension in your body. If you have previous knowledge of the Tarot, breathe this out as well while you come completely present. Let your mind be open and receptive when you approach the cards because you will then have more room to explore!

When your mind is still, open your eyes and look at the card. Allow your being to drink in the vibration of the card through your eyes. Do not try to understand or engage your mind around the card; simply experience it visually. Notice if you feel attracted to the card or uncomfortable with it. What does it evoke inside of you? Again, keep releasing anything that you "know" and dream the card freshly.

To deepen your experience, now dream yourself into the card. Close your eyes and visualize yourself as the card's main figure. What would it feel like to be stepping towards the edge of the cliff as the Fool or swinging upside down as the Hanged One? Use your imagination to bring the card to life around you. Activate all of your senses. What smells, tactile sensations, and sounds can you perceive? How does it feel to embody the energy of the card from the inside out? As you become the card, let its energy permeate your being and inform your cells.

POETRY

The qualities of each card are embodied in a poem that contains the "art" of the card, as well as few keywords to anchor the drawing into words. Before you read the overview or symbology of the cards, sit quietly and absorb the poem. Different parts of your brain are activated as you read the card's poem silently and out loud. Open yourself to feeling the energy of the card through the words.

OVERVIEW

Once you have absorbed the textures of the card through its images and poetry, the overview will give you a deeper intellectual understanding of the card. As you read, keep opening up and listening between the lines. Move beyond intellectual reading, into tasting and digesting the words. Who do you know who seems to emanate the energies of this card? Is the card familiar or disturbing? Would you like more of this card's energies in your life or less? Why? Don't just roll the answers around in your head, but feel into your body for them.

EXCESS/DEFICIENCY

The Tarot contains no "good" or "bad" cards. However, we can be in balance or out of balance with the energy of a card. Balance naturally occurs when we refrain from either extreme of a particular energy. Working with excess/deficiency portion allows you to ascertain if you are off-center by holding too much or too little of an archetypal pattern. This assessment will lead you to more actively use the cards in your life by exploring how you can create harmony within yourself. Often another card will assist you to relieve excess or deficiencies. For example, if you have an excess of Empress energy, it would be beneficial to work with the Emperor card to summon more structure and discipline. When you find imbalances, feel through the other cards to find an antidote. What can you put into action to integrate the fullest expression of each card into your being?

SYMBOLS

To deepen your intellectual understanding of the cards, all main symbols are listed and briefly described. Read the symbol definitions one at a time, and then locate the symbol in the image. Feel the meaning of the symbol in your body, rather than simply thinking about it. Make it your own, moving it beyond concept and into reality. For example, in the Magician card, roses are a symbol of passion. Find where the roses are positioned in relation to the Magician, and then use all of your senses to bring them to life. How do roses evoke the qualities of desire and passion within you? Evoke their smell, taste, touch, color, and discover how they connect to your own passion. The wand represents the Will of the Magician and his connection between Earth and Sky. Find the wand in the picture, and then imagine yourself holding a wand. How would it feel in your hand? Relish the sensation of the wand connecting you to Earth and Sky.

HEBREW ALPHABET

Tarot has long been associated with the Hebrew alphabet, which contains twenty-two letters, the same number as the major arcana. Each letter represents a picture, which was first noted in the Zohar, a primary Kabalistic text. In 1781, the Comte de Mellet wrote publicly on the link between the Tarot and the Hebrew letters. Since then, several interpretations have described the alignment between the Tarot and the Hebrew alphabet. I have chosen to associate each card with a specific Hebraic letter, for example, the Fool with the first Hebraic letter Aleph. Each description of the Hebrew letter will give you more insight into the card, and the Hebraic symbols are in themselves powerful tools to use in dreaming. Notice how the letter represents the form of its meaning.

COLORING

Coloring the cards is a means to imprint them deeper into your psyche and to make the cards your own. I tell my students to color the cards two times — one in the traditional manner outlined with each card, and then again in whatever creative way most delights them. We have used colored pencils, markers, watercolor, tempura, glitter pens, crayons, and other media to color the cards. Remember this is sacred play! Free your inner child, and do not be afraid to color outside of the lines. Let the coloring aspect be a joy, not a chore. Stay soft and slow as you allow each color to inform your subconsciousness and deepen your connection with the card. This is not a race or a competition!

If you want to leave your original cards black and white, you can make a photocopy of the image on cardstock and paint on this. Some people enjoy enlarging the cards, so they have more space to color. I have consciously omitted hair and skin color, so you can choose these aspects of the card. Create diversity!

Each color has a certain energetic vibration that corresponds with a specific meaning or element. These keys are taken from the now out of print *Keystone of Tarot Symbols*.

White: Purity, Spirit, element of Ether.
Yellow: Mental body, intellect, element of Air.
Red: Energetic body, action, courage, strength, element of Fire.
Orange: Positive energy and vitality, authority, blend of Air and Fire energies.
Green: Growth, increase, desire, abundance.
Blue: Receptivity, reflection, memory, element of Water.
Violet: Spiritual Truth and vision.
Brown: Earthiness.
Black: Primal matter, the unknown, element of Earth.
Gray: Wisdom, perfect blend of black and white, non-duality.
Silver: Lunar energy.
Gold: Solar energy.

TOLTEC TAROT MYTHOLOGY

Three masteries comprise the Toltec path: the Mastery of Awareness, the Mastery of Transformation, and the Mastery of Intent. Awareness is the foundation, and it encourages us to uncover our agreements, habits, and patterning so we may live more fully in choice. Awareness gives us the tools, but it alone is not enough. The Mastery of Transformation invites us to step up and to use these tools to create change in an inner alchemical process of deepening. The Mastery of Intent, or Love, unfolds naturally once we have transformed fear into acceptance. At this level, we harbor no resistance or fear, and our Intent manifests effortlessly. Our experience of the world flows naturally from the depths of gratitude.

Don Miguel Ruiz beautifully writes in his book, *The Mastery of Love*, "When we master Awareness, Transformation, and Love, we reclaim our divinity and become one with God. This is the goal of the Toltec."

The Toltec Tarot mirrors the three Toltec masteries. Cards 0 to 11 evoke the energies necessary to master our awareness. Cards 12 to 19 reflect the Mastery of Transformation, and this series of cards carries us through a multilayered Toltec initiation ceremony at Teotihuacán, Mexico. Cards 20 and 21 reflect the Mastery of Intent and reveal the beauty of living in co-creation with the Divine.

CARDS 0 TO 11, FOOL TO JUSTICE: MASTERY OF AWARENESS

The symbols for these cards derive from many different spiritual traditions. Each card gifts us with an expanded consciousness and a diversity of tools for gathering energy and awareness. The Fool begins the process with his willingness to step off the cliff of the known and to move towards the balance of Justice.

0 - FOOL: Joy and the power of faith in walking your path. Learning how to laugh at yourself. Keyword: Purity! Bring innocence and curiosity into all aspects of life.

1 - MAGICIAN: The power of focus and discipline. Learning to manifest your Intent. Keyword: Mastery! To make changes in your life, you must take conscious action.

2 - HIGH PRIESTESS: The tools of stillness and internal depth. Learning to trust your inner knowing. Keyword: Silence. Plunge beneath the known into the waters of the unknown.

3 - EMPRESS: The power of abundance and beauty. Learning to expand and love all things with an open heart. Keyword: Birth. Let all possibilities blossom fully.

4 - EMPEROR: The power of form and discipline. Learning to set limits and to define your edges. Keyword: Boundary. Create structure to support the core gift.

Toltec Tarot Mythology

5 - HIEROPHANT: The power of spiritual community. Learning how to connect to inner and outer guidance. Keyword: Linkage. Weaving Spirit back into form.

6 - LOVERS: The power of opposites coming together. Learning how to honor and blend all aspects. of our self. Keyword: Unify. Not looking outside of ourselves for completion.

7 - CHARIOT: The power of balancing mind and emotions. Learning how to step beyond convention. Keyword: Intent. Taking action to manifest your goals.

8 - STRENGTH: The power of embracing our internal fears. Learning to ride our passion and animal nature. Keyword: Fierceness. Feeling our internal fire.

9 - HERMIT: The power of retreat for internal healing. Learning how to find our Light and how to bring it back into the world. Keyword: Illumination. Accessing our inner stillness.

10 - WHEEL OF FORTUNE: The power of trusting the process of transformation. Learning to surrender to the ups and downs of human existence. Keyword: Turning. Honoring the cycles of life.

11 - JUSTICE: The power of trusting the law of cause and effect. Learning to perceive beyond "right" and "wrong." Keyword: Balance. Witnessing the results of your actions.

CARDS 12 TO 19, HANGED ONE TO SUN: MASTERY OF TRANSFORMATION

The symbols for these cards spring from a time-honored initiation ceremony that has been experienced by thousands of people at the ancient pyramid complex of Teotihuacán, Mexico. This heart of Toltec wisdom bestows a series of challenges that encourage initiates to move beyond fears and limitations to embrace their fullest potential and to reclaim their individual ray of Light. Each card in this series portrays a different phase of the transformational process. When we walk this transformational path in Teotihuacán, we work directly with the site while passing through two cards a day at each of the gateways of transformation.

This initiation sequence is described in don Miguel's book, *Beyond Fear*. We have slightly adjusted the traditional process to balance action with inspiration.

The journey begins as the Hanged One surrenders to a greater power, and the initiation process culminates in a final celebratory ceremony at the Pyramid of the Sun. Our path involves facing the difficult truths of our lives while being inspired to dismantle our old inhibiting structures. Each card offers a transformation action and its keyword.

12 - HANGED ONE: The gift of surrendering what no longer serves you. Before you can enter the mystery of Teotihuacán, you must first let go of your "island of safety," all the concepts of whom you believe you are and who

you are supposed to be in the world. Keyword: Reversal. Transformational Action: Willingness to surrender false beliefs. Willingness is the first requisite step in transformation.

13 - DEATH: This is the point of no return, when we face the Angel of Death in order to release the body and any temptation to remain fixated in our old self. Only those who have completely surrendered and are unafraid can pass through the gateway guarded by the Angel of Death. In Teotihuacán, this pathway is called the Avenue of the Dead. Keyword: Dissolution. Being willing to die to everything you know to claim your authentic self. Transformational Action: Symbolically burying our body in the earth and attending our own funeral. Dying to our old self opens the doors of transformation.

14 - TEMPERANCE: Once we have died to all that we know, we taste what is to come. This card depicts the Butterfly Palace in Teotihuacán and the power of temperance to rebirth ourselves anew. The nectar of Spirit inspires us to blossom and find the sweetness of our emotions and passions. Keyword: Butterfly. Here we are inspired and filled with blessings to face the hard work that our travels of transformation entails. Transformational Action: Knowing that all of life's difficulties can serve to prepare us to fully unfurl our wings and fly. Embracing life's struggles as gifts accelerates our transformation.

15 - DEVIL: The portal in Teotihuacán represents a major gateway since this is where the Masters traveled psychically.

All possibilities await us, but we are prevented from touching infinity by the Devil in the form of self-punishment, judgments, and fears. Keyword: Adversary. Transformational Action: Facing our Devil with compassion and breaking free of its negative voice. Acceptance of our shadow-side transforms fears into faith and compassion, allowing us to glimpse God.

16 - TOWER: After facing the Devil and making a new choice, we return with new inspiration to the Avenue of the Dead. Here we intend to let go of any aspects of ourselves that hinder us from not just glimpsing, but actually embodying God. Each plaza along the Avenue of the Dead invites us to shatter all aspects of self, as we release our body, emotions, mind, and Spirit. Keyword: Lightning. Transformational Action: Taking responsibility (without judgment!) for how our thoughts, words, and actions create distracting drama and chaos in our lives.

17 - STAR: After the destructive, irrevocable energy of the Tower, we travel to the Women's Temple in Teotihuacán. Here we reflect on our true Light and call in healing energy to fill the spaces opened during our walk down the Avenue of the Dead. The permeating, comforting energy of the Women's Temple feeds our soul. Here, we realize who we are beyond our old stories and beliefs. The well in the temple mirrors back to us our own unique essence, just as the water reflects the Star's true face. Keyword: Nourishment. Transformational Action: After difficult times, we savor quiet space to nourish and refuel our spirits and to bask in our authentic Light.

18 - MOON: With renewed energy from the Star card and a new sense of freedom following the dissolution of our ego Tower, we continue down the Avenue of the Dead towards the Pyramid of the Moon. This temple, which beckoned to us from over Death's shoulder, connects us back to our primal, instinctual nature. To access its power in Teotihuacán, as we walk to a platform in front of the Pyramid of the Moon, we create an "energetic double," an etheric copy of all our experiences, thoughts, and being. At the Moon plaza we dive into Mystery with a final surrender of all that we thought we were by releasing our double to the infinite. Keyword: Depth. Transformational Action: Embracing our animal nature and instincts.

19 - SUN: At the Pyramid of the Moon, we reconnect to our sacred animal nature by releasing all that we know and even our concept of humanness. Beyond words and thoughts, we then travel to and ascend the Pyramid of the Sun to reclaim our divine nature. By connecting to the Sun, we awaken to our true purpose in life: to celebrate and radiate our Light brightly. Keyword: Illumination. Transformational Action: Readily stepping forward to share our gifts with the world.

CARDS 20 AND 21, JUDGMENT AND COSMOS: MASTERY OF INTENT

With the first eleven cards, Fool through Justice, we gain awareness and insights. With the following eight cards, Hanged One to Sun, we absorb what we have learned and put it into action, transforming our reality. The final two cards of the Major Arcana, Judgment and Cosmos, encapsulate the energy of transcendence, the Mastery of Love.

20 - JUDGMENT: As we gain awareness and energy, we increase our ability to make conscious choice. We see the places where we sabotage, victimize, and judge ourselves with our thoughts and actions. We recognize where we use others' perspectives and judgments to hurt ourselves. We stop blaming or whining or criticizing and start to experience the world from a totally different point of view. Keyword: Awakening. The Judgment card marks the joyous day when we gain the energy and grace to step out of our restrictive self-concepts to consistently see ourselves through the eyes of God.

21 - COSMOS: In the Cosmos card, we have returned to the innocence of the Fool, and we now also embody mature wisdom in our dance. We live beyond duality and separation, immersed in the sweetness of the Divine. We awaken to our true nature, which is beyond mind, emotions, and physical form. Keyword: Completion. Here we walk in the world knowing that we are the perfect seamless blend of animal, human, and Divine. We realize that our being is eternal and sacred, as is all of life.

The Toltec Tarot

Major Arcana

Fool

Purity

I am sweet joyous abandon
dancing into the Mystery
with heart open wide.
My art is ecstatic innocence.
I walk without fear of
failure or success,
every step a prayer.
I carry everything I need.
The fire in my heart leads the way,
my feet firmly implanted in the Now.
Nothing can hold me back
as I gleefully
Jump!
From the edge
Of any limits.

I am the grateful Fool.

0 – The Fool

OVERVIEW

The Fool reminds us of the joy of open-minded innocence. Whenever we step off the cliff of the known, we enter a dimension of exploration without attachment. As we commit to move beyond our previous conscious and unconscious agreements and belief systems, we must journey with a light heart, a sense of humor, patience, and a passionate desire to live in Truth.

Each step on our travels is a return to the authentic self — the foolish, in-the-moment self. I am that I am. With the Fool, we embody a total acceptance of self. We envision ourselves as a unique ray of Light, as a sacred seed of possibility.

When we call upon Fool energy, we invite in the wisdom of no-mind and the pure guidance of the unseen. We cannot always explain our actions and impulses, yet we implicitly trust them. Each step we take comes from a sense of sacred play and mystical joy.

This card is powered by forward momentum, although this momentum lacks a defined destination or goal. It is a pilgrimage to the unknown, an adventure into ourselves that we undertake with perfect trust in divine guidance. We may struggle or resist or go into fear. Yet our Intent to return to our own center and to live in the present moment propels us off the cliffs of our limiting beliefs, until we learn to open our wings and fly.

When you have a DEFICIENCY of Fool energy, you probably
- Take life and yourself much too seriously
- Have strong attachments to how things should look and unfold

When you have an EXCESS of Fool energy, you probably
- Do not have the focus or will to finish projects or deepen relationships
- Use compulsive risk taking or distraction to avoid your emotions or responsibilities

SYMBOLS to help you dream the Fool card:

POUCH
This container holds all the wisdom accumulated from the Fool's journey, from both past lives and present learning.

FEATHER AND BIRD
These symbols of wisdom evoke clear, bird's-eye perception.

COMPANION DOG
"Man's best friend" represents the Fool's instinctual, animal self, but even the dog is left behind as the Fool steps off the cliff.

ROSE
The white rose symbolizes purity and innocence.

Fool

HEBREW LETTER: ALEPH / BULL

The powerful bull is an ancient magical symbol of sensuality and art. It reflects the Fool's inherent strength and his sensuous, feeling nature. Aleph is the root letter that all other Hebrew letters emanate from, and it is the only letter in the Hebrew alphabet that makes no sound of its own in a word.

FOOL COLORING INSTRUCTIONS

White: Collar of shirt and two long strips of cloth on either side of vest, hose, dog, rose, snow on mountain peaks, eye on flap of pouch, point on bottom of staff, sun and rays, first circle around sun, edges of clouds.
Yellow: Radiance around sun, two circles on garment, clouds, boots.
Green: Designs on outer garment, bottom edge of garment, leaves on rose, wreath around head, collar, edge of sash, buttons on boots.
Blue: Sleeves, inside of vest, and bottom of garment, mountains (light, white snow)
Red: Feather, lining on inner edge of sleeves, spokes on wheels, pouch (except for button and eye), dog's tongue.
Brown: Grass and cliff, leggings (tan).
Black: Staff, (except knob).
Silver: Moon on vest.
Gold: Metal on bottom of staff (point is white), belt.

Mastery

I am fierce focus,
An unending channel
between Earth and Sky.
My art is Creative Intent,
to use my will
to cut
through any limitation
to create the impossible
with magical thinking
and sacred action.
My roots sing in the earth,
My branches entwine with the clouds.
My Will is aligned with
Divine
Creation.

I am the adept Magician.

1 - Magician

OVERVIEW

The Magician is pure Intent in action. When we align with this energy, we know that every thought, movement, and feeling affects our personal dream and the larger consensual dream around us. We choose to take complete responsibility for ourselves and to support our alchemical transformation, which purifies fear into Light.

"As above, so below" is the Magician's motto. All our actions in the physical, mundane world affect the spiritual realms; and the spirit work we do also affects our physical world. We can use ritual to link the mundane with the spiritual. When we perform ritual and ceremony, we become a channel linking worlds together, a bridge between the physical and spiritual.

The Magician is the shaman, one who travels to the spiritual realm to gather information and healing energies to bring back to the community. The stillness and focus of the Magician and his easy access to his "tools" on the table before him, remind us of the great benefit of clearing confusion and doubt from our being. We step into our integrity and innate power as we release our need for others to like us, and our fear of our own power.

Don Miguel Ruiz placed the Magician as the last of the major arcana to emphasize that much work is required to truly hold this card. Our journey through the Tarot moves from the innocence of the Fool to the accumulated wisdom and commitment of the Magician.

When you have a DEFICIENCY of Magician energy, you probably
- Do not make clear decisions
- Are afraid of your power

When you have an EXCESS of Magician energy, you probably
- Are narrowly focused on your goal
- Use your energy to run over people

SYMBOLS to help you dream the Magician card:

FOUR ELEMENTS
Each tool represents one of the four elements as Spirit manifest in form. The sword is air, the wand is fire, the chalice is water, and the coins are earth.

ROSES
The red roses symbolize passion and intensity.

WAND
The uplifted wand represents the Magician's Will and his connection to both Earth and Sky.

INFINITY SYMBOL
The infinity sign demonstrates that the Magician's vision is firmly planted in the infinite. One half represents Earth and the forces of creativity, while the other half represents Sky and the forces of Intent. The center where they meet is Creative Intent, the perfect balance of flow and focus.

Ouroboros, the snake swallowing its tail, symbolizes the unending circle of life, which surrounds and informs the Magician.

HEBREW LETTER: BETH / HOUSE
The Magician is full and a house unto himself. The four elements are the cornerstones of his personal house. The Magician creates physical manifestation as a dwelling for the Divine.

MAGICIAN COLORING INSTRUCTIONS
White: Sleeves and main garment, hood of cloak, head band, (except circle and wings), infinity sign, shaft of wand on table and in Magician's hand.
Red: Robe (wraps around front and back), design and edge of sleeves, and roses.
Yellow: Stars and moon, trees, top of wand on table.
Green: Foliage.
Blue/Green: Serpent belt, liquid in cup.
Brown: Table.
Silver: Stem of cup, highlights on main cup, pentagram traced on coin, circle on headband.
Gold: Sword handle, end of wand shaft on table and in hand, coins on table (except pentagram), wings on headband.
Gray: Sword blade (dark gray).

High Priestess

Silence

I am the veil between the worlds.
My vision spans the boundaries
between form and formlessness.
My art is to flow beneath illusion,
beneath duality.
No words, no thoughts, no doubts –
Intuiting
the whisper of
Truth
in each flicker of fire,
within each drop of water.
My gaze touches all things.
From the seen
to the unseen,
nothing is hidden.

I am the intuitive High Priestess.

2 - The High Priestess

OVERVIEW

The High Priestess is the receptive counterpart to the active energy of the Magician. She embodies the subconscious mysteries and our ability to tap deeply into the waters of our own intuition and mystical knowing. Like the Magician, she stands between worlds, bridging manifest and unmanifest energies.

Linked to the ever-changing Moon, the High Priestess is the sovereign of our unconscious realms, whereas the Magician (allied with the Sun) embodies pure consciousness. The High Priestess challenges us to travel into the depths, to move beyond our mind or will and to surrender to a greater flow.

While we may be fearful of our unconscious selves, and our unseen beliefs, great power resides in these dark places. The High Priestess reminds us to sink into the silence of the subconscious, beneath the fear and chaos that may be hiding there. When we move deeper into these hidden places, we discover the universal collective unconscious to be a resplendent source of information and compassion for all beings.

This card invites us to let go of our familiar circumstances and to travel behind the curtain of the known. It calls us to enter a place where we are challenged to embrace the oceanic song of life. Here, our definitions hold no sway. In this realm our heart learns to see with new ears and our belly opens to taste new visions.

When you have a DEFICIENCY of Priestess energy, you probably
- Do not trust your intuition or have it confused with your destructive impulses
- Are afraid of your depth

When you have an EXCESS of Priestess energy, you probably
- Are aloof and difficult to connect with
- Live through dreams and feelings in an ungrounded way

SYMBOLS to help you dream the High Priestess card:

PILLARS
She stands between duality, serving as a neutral bridge. The white pillar represents "yod," yes, positive energy, and the element of fire. The black pillar represents "beth," no, negative energy, and the element of water.

MOON
The Priestess's headdress shows the waning, full, and waxing moons. She receives guidance from the reflective silvery moon, which shines on her beyond the curtains.

CURTAIN
The curtain in the background reminds us of the veil between the worlds. The musical notes on the walls show another bridge from Spirit to matter.

High Priestess

POMEGRANATE AND SCROLL
The Priestess holds a pomegranate and a scroll in her hands. This fruit is an ancient symbol of death and rebirth, the creative force of the cycles of life. The scroll contains the akashic records and memories of all human experience.

CROSS
The necklace contains the perfect balance of the male (vertical line) with female (horizontal line), echoing the union of Spirit and matter.

HEBREW LETTER: GIMEL / CAMEL
The High Priestess is self-sufficient. Like the camel, she contains the water that nourishes her through any journey.

HIGH PRIESTESS COLORING INSTRUCTIONS
White: Inner garment and left sleeve, left side of robe, cross on breast, veil on head, right pillar, small house on left pillar, stars on robe, side walls.
Yellow: Flame atop right pillar.
Blue: Panels and designs on center and right side of robe (create a sense of flowing water), very inner edge of hood, water in bowl on left pillar, mountains outside window, curtains, musical notes.
Green: Greenery outside window.
Red: Pomegranate (seeds deeper red), cener of flame.
Brown: Scroll (tan).
Gray: Stones in floor and back wall.
Silver: Headpiece, moon and rays in background.

Empress

3

The Empress

Birth

I am ecstatic abundance
celebrating all creation
without distinction.
My art is to midwife all possibility
with pure acceptance
and a mother's overflowing "yes!"
Blessing each tiny bud,
nourishing every seed.
My heart blossoms
wings that whisper
to every aspect of creation,
"Grow, child, grow.
Unfurl your being.
Trust deeply.
Love all."

I am the bountiful Empress.

3 - Empress

OVERVIEW

The Empress teaches us how to open to everything. She embodies pure abundance and unconditional acceptance from an overflowing well of love. The Empress opens her heart to all around her, loving all beings without judgment or needing them to change. This acceptance of others emanates from a full acceptance of self.

The Empress invites us to open our eyes and being to the abundance that encompasses us and to live in love rather than in scarcity or fear. We make this transition by feeling sincere thankfulness for what we have. When we focus on what we are grateful for, rather than what is missing, we consciously shift our perspective away from scarcity and into fullness and plenty. This also strengthens our ability to tap into our creative self.

Through the Empress, we come to know that we are inherently linked to all of creation. From this wisdom, we can rest in the luxuriant beauty that exists within and without. As we reconnect to the bounty of the Earth, we encourage our creativity to flow without hindrance from our mind or limiting belief structures.

Yes! All things are possible when we remember our innate wholeness and honor the dance of life in every moment, every creature, and every ray of sunshine. The Empress does not control her emotions or fear her cycles; she opens with equanimity to all expressions of life, without preconceived conditions.

When you have a DEFICIENCY of Empress energy, you probably
- Live in your head, separate from your body
- Do not feel abundance or a sense of creative flow

When you have an EXCESS of Empress energy, you probably
- Have a difficult time setting boundaries
- Tend towards care taking and being a martyr

SYMBOLS to help you dream the Empress card:

STAFF
The Empress holds a staff that symbolizes her sovereignty over herself and her dream. The cross on top reflects the balance of Spirit and matter, while the orb represents the world.

NECKLACE
Above her heart, the necklace contains a winged heart, showing that she is protected by the fierce openness of her heart. The flying birds echo this energetic.

WATERFALL
Flowing water brings life and energy as it courses through the land.

FRUIT AND FLOWERS
Colorful plants represent abundance and fruition of the seed.

CREATIVE FORCE

The twelve stars on her head reflect her connection to the creative fire of the universe. Her pregnant belly links her to the Earth's fertility. The snake crawling out of her staff establishes her connection to the Earth and to the cycles of renewal as it periodically sheds its skin to reveal new life.

HEBREW LETTER: DALETH / DOOR

Honors the Empress as a portal for life. She is the gateway that births all things, the doorway that opens for diversity to enter.

EMPRESS COLORING INSTRUCTIONS

White: Wings of heart on necklace, highlights in waterfall, birds, cuff of bracelet and anklet, rays of light from the sun.
Yellow: Sun and sky, staff handle, flowers on the ground, tops of mountains, blanket mixed with green.
Blue: Waterfall and stream.
Green: Foliage, grass, snake, fringe and decoration on bracelet and anklet, ball on scepter (not bar and cross), hills in foreground, blanket swirls mixed with yellow.
Red: Fruit, blossoms in tree, heart in necklace, snake tongue.
Brown: Tree trunks, rocks near waterfall.
Gray: Pillow she reclines against, rocks.
Gold: Stars, cross on ball and scepter, earring.

The Emperor

Boundary

I am visionary discernment,
the power of sacred limits
and unbiased decisions.
My art is to establish the lines
that strengthen the core
and hone the purpose
of each action.
I protect what is fruitful
and weed what no longer serves.
Conscious structure is my mandate,
Discipline is my grace –
Not to limit,
but to fully free
the Spirit seed
from chaff.

I am the warrior Emperor.

4 - The Emperor

OVERVIEW

The Empress teaches us abundance; the Emperor teaches us structure. Both aspects are vitally important on a spiritual path. Without the wisdom and discerning energy of the Emperor, we would never let go of any agreement, relationship, or object. This royal warrior gifts us with the clarity to determine what will best serve us and the inner strength to release everything else.

This card teaches us to shift the way we perceive through our window (perception) using structure and discipline to illicit the truth of each situation. The Emperor is a master at discernment. When we discern, we simply see what is, without judgment. From this place of witness, we can make good choices and learn from our missteps.

The Emperor establishes firm boundaries that allow love to flourish. We abuse ourselves when we do not set boundaries due to fear of hurting others or of being abandoned. When we set a boundary from our center, we create space for more self-love and honesty. This principle also applies to defining internal boundaries with any aspect of our self that does not serve our growth.

The Emperor's view is not clouded with stories or old emotions. This fosters great vision and insight. He teaches us to look at a situation from many perspectives, to creatively move beyond our usual perceptual mode and to seek out bold new solutions. Great awareness and presence are the Emperor's gifts to us on our healing journey.

When you have a DEFICIENCY of Emperor energy, you probably
- Are spacey and unpredictable
- Have a difficult time structuring your life

When you have an EXCESS of Emperor energy, you probably
- Have a need to understand and control the world around you
- Are strongly judgmental

SYMBOLS to help you dream the Emperor:

RAM
The ram on the Emperor's chest is a symbol of action and focus on the end result.

SQUARE
The Emperor rests on a square base, reflecting the power of structure and clear boundaries. His foundation is solid and defined.

SHIELD
His shield rests at his side because the Emperor-warrior uses his Will and Intent for protection, not weapons or armor. His energy is aligned with divine Will.

GLOBE AND SCEPTOR
The globe represents the world, and the Emperor's support

of physical and spiritual growth (cross on top of globe.) The scepter is topped by an ankh, a symbol of life, and shows his willingness to protect what is precious to him.

HEBREW LETTER: HEH / WINDOW
The Hebrew symbol for this card is a window. This window represents how the Emperor creates a framework to focus his view and choices.

EMPEROR COLORING INSTRUCTIONS
White: Ram's head on chest, piping on vest, border of inverted T on globe in right hand, inside of shield (except design and border).
Yellow: Handle of scepter, sun and rays.
Blue: Stream.
Green: Grass atop the cliff.
Red: Mountains, design and edge of shield, globe in left hand (except inverted T and cross).
Orange: Sky.
Violet: Belt (except white border), outer garment (except insignia on left shoulder, piping, and cloth around shoulders).
Brown: Cliff, land by stream.
Gray: Stone cube, cuffs around wrist, cloth around shoulders. Boots and breastplate are dark gray.
Gold: Inverted T and cross of globe.

Hierophant

5

Hierophant

Linkage

I am velvet Truth,
the voice of Spirit, calling you home
to yourself.
My art is to awaken your inner God/dess,
with a whisper
or a shout.
I reconnect your self
to the soul of infinity,
reminding you of what
you truly are.
Listen, can you hear
your own unique song?
Join the choir,
singing praises
to the One.

I am the illuminating Hierophant.

5 - Hierophant

OVERVIEW

The Hierophant connects us to Spirit as the "one who shows or brings the Light." We can experience this energy in people who hold the role of teacher or mentor; we also can attune ourselves to our inner Hierophant, our own divine voice. Hierophants can be gurus, priests, spiritual teachers, healers, rabbis, or any inspirational being.

The Hierophant shares the wisdom of deep listening — calling on our highest spiritual selves to listen, nourish, and guide our child-personality self back to a remembrance of our infinite connection to Spirit. This card reflects different aspects of ourselves: the Hierophant is our Highest Self; and the twin disciples of purity and desire are aspects of our personality.

We often mistakenly transfer our power to teachers or mentors (or partners or bosses...) hoping they will fix or make everything better, instead of recognizing them as reflections of our own Highest Self. Good guides are a precious gift. Use your guides as models to support you in recapturing your own wisdom.

Another common pitfall is to empower your internal victim/judge voices. How many times have you listened to your victim or judge and believed they were trustworthy guides? These are false hierophants, demanding that you relinquish your Light to remain safe and small. Keep listening beyond their insistent voices for your true guidance.

When you have a DEFICIENCY of the Hierophant energy, you probably
- Listen to and act out the petty voices within
- Do not trust anyone to hold a clear reflection

When you have an EXCESS of Hierophant energy, you probably
- Believe you are foolproof and wise when your ego is actually running the show
- Keep searching for the perfect guru to fix you

SYMBOLS to help you dream the Hierophant card:

DISCIPLES
One disciple represents purity and discipline; the other is desire and energy. The path to Spirit is through these dual doorways of Will and surrender, stalker and dreamer, focus and expansion.

HAND GESTURE
The Hierophant raises his left hand to the sky with two fingers upraised, signifying unity and conscious community. His right fingers point to the Earth, reflecting the individual quest to embrace the unconscious shadow-self.

HOOD
The Hierophant's hood demonstrates that he cloaks himself from the critical voice of judgment and tunes his ears to the whispers of the Divine.

KEY

The central key suggests the direct transmission of Spirit via the Hierophant by means of a non-verbal energetic channel that connects the disciples directly to Source. It is positioned between the disciples, showing that the key is a non-dual element lying beyond purity and desire.

HEBREW LETTER: VOV / HOOK

This Hebrew letter means "link or hook" and is associated with the word "and." The Hierophant is the link to Spirit, the connecting force between physical and ethereal.

HIEROPHANT COLORING INSTRUCTIONS

White: Shirt and trim inside sleeves, front trim of robe, edge of pants of disciples' clothing, caps on heads of disciples, clothing of disciple on right, circle around disciples' heads, clouds and streaks on mountains.
Yellow: Edge of hood and inside folds, symbol on chest.
Red: Hood and cloak, robe, and rose on disciple at left.
Green: Leaf of rose.
Blue: Shirt under robe, belt of disciple on right.
Silver: Crescent at throat, box holding key, moon in sky.
Gold: Key.
Gray: Pillars behind Hierophant, mountains.

Lovers

6

The Lovers

Unify

I am Earth and Sky –
Opposites merging,
Flesh made Spirit, Spirit made flesh.
My art is sacred union,
to show the two they are one
and that the One is everything.
I take you beyond knowledge
or story
or form
To see through the eyes of the Angel
to witness the Truth –
The lover does not wait outside of you
but within,
waiting for the sacred marriage
of you to you.

I am the unending Lovers.

6 ~ Lovers

OVERVIEW

The Lovers card depicts the maturation of our inner alchemy. To find inner wholeness, we must stop searching outside of ourselves for completion. We must take responsibility for reconnecting the indwelling trinity of our subconscious, conscious, and superconscious aspects.

The figure on the left represents Earth energy — receptive, open, and expansive. The figure on the right represents Sky energy — active, focused, and present. Spirit reminds us that these two aspects of self are not separate, but two polarities that when merged transport us to our Angel self.

Most of us have a natural affinity towards the Earth essence or the Sky essence. Yet it requires a commitment to strengthen and heal both Earth and Sky energies within for us to attain the balance of the Lovers. When we look outside of ourselves for completion, we bind ourselves with cords of attachment and fear instead of opening unconditionally to Spirit.

The Lovers card explores the story of Adam and Eve, Toltec style. Whenever we believe ourselves to be separate, we have eaten the apple and our ego begins to try to understand everything around us. We fabricate stories based on our limited knowledge to give ourselves a sense of safety. To come back into alignment, we must embrace the Tree of Life that shimmers within the flame of Truth.

When you have a DEFICIENCY of the Lovers energy, you probably
- Are cynical and bitter
- Fight to keep your individuality intact at the cost of relationships

When you have an EXCESS of Lovers energy, you probably
- Are caught in romantic fantasy and look outside of yourself for someone to complete you
- Fight to keep relationships intact at the cost of the individuals

SYMBOLS to help you dream the Lovers card:

ANGEL
The angelic figure is Archangel Raphael, the Angel of healing. He stands for the superconscious part of our self that heals all separation by connecting directly to divinity. Raphael embraces all of our being and creates a doorway for our rebirth and renewal.

TREES
On the left is the Tree of Knowledge, on the right the Tree of Life. To live fully, we must balance our knowledge with our direct experience of the world, blending human rational thought and animal intuition.

ROSE
The red flower between the Lovers is a symbol of their passion.

HAND GESTURES

The Lovers face each other with open hearts and with open hands. They do not grasp or try to control one other. They honor and respect their differences and celebrate individuality, which allows love to flow unimpeded by fear or need.

HEBREW LETTER: ZAIN / SWORD

The sword is a single blade with two sides. When we embody the Lovers card, we cut through all illusion of separation. We remember ourselves as a transcendental soul cloaked in a physical body.

LOVERS COLORING INSTRUCTIONS

White: Breath and cloud, Angel's collar, clouds around mountains, inner arch.
Yellow: Flames with red inside, sun, inside bracelets of figure on right.
Red: Angel's wings with purple highlights, fruit, flame highlights, rose, face of arch, jewel and outside bracelets on arm of figure on right.
Blue: Sky below Angel (with violet rays), stream, alternate rays from sun.
Green: Foreground, foothills, foliage, serpent, jewel and anklet of figure on left.
Violet: Angel's garments, tops of wings and feather highlights, mountains (more diluted), rays from sun and Angel (alternating with blue).
Brown: Left tree trunk.
Gray: Right tree trunk (dark).
Gold: Sun above Angel, and lines from sun.

Chariot

7

Chariot

Intent

I am the arrow's flight
and the wind which carries the arrow
and the hand which guides the arrow.
My art is to ride in the center
of all movement, using my tools
to be arrow, wind, hand, and goal.
I glide away from the known world
perfectly balancing the fulcrum
of mind with body, emotions with Spirit.
I chart my own course.
The path of mastery cultivates
the mastery of path.
In flight, like the arrow,
I have already
reached my destination.

I am the dynamic Chariot.

7 - Chariot

OVERVIEW

The Charioteer leaves what is familiar behind and moves with grace beyond the structure of town (socialization). His calm face and his energetic rather than physical connection to the reins show us how we can balance our emotional and mental bodies by using clear focused Intent to guide us forward.

Driving a chariot is a balancing act. All experiences, "good" and "bad," assist in learning self-mastery by helping us to witness where we are off balance in our lives. Your actions and thoughts steer your own physical chariot, so it is crucial to set Intent to maintain forward momentum.

The Chariot teaches us to gather our tools and to use them appropriately. Spending our lives simply gathering tools will slow our progress. Attempting to change old patterns and behaviors with insufficient or ineffective tools will spin us in circles. Thoroughly embodying the resources you possess and integrating them into your life allows you to gain mastery over mind and emotions.

This is a card of ACTION! that stems from a calm center and the willingness to move beyond limitations. The Charioteer honors the past and chooses the future in each moment. He is ever aware and constantly makes course corrections. The more quickly you are willing to readjust your attitude, the faster you will travel.

When you have a DEFICIENCY of the Chariot energy, you probably
- Are unskilled at balancing your emotions and mental bodies
- Have lots of tools but do not actively use them

When you have an EXCESS of Chariot energy, you probably
- Allow no room for surprises or mistakes in your life
- Do not stop to enjoy the view on your journey

SYMBOLS to help you dream the Chariot card:

TWO HORSES
Black and white, the horses convey that we can see our destination clearly only when we transcend duality and have the will to guide ourselves. If the Charioteer allows either animal (body or mind, emotions or Spirit) to race out of control, it will wildly run him off course. He uses his vision and openhearted focus to keep distractions and drama reined in and wisely harnesses their energy to move forward.

FOUR PILLARS
Four pillars, representing the four elements, hold up the canopy and protect the charioteer on his journey. These four pillars show he has a strong foundation that allows him to react quickly and fluidly to all changes, while steadily maintaining his course.

OVERHEAD CANOPY
The canopy represents the protection and guidance of Spirit, sheltering the Charioteer.

BIRD AND CHALICE
The eagle carrying the chalice symbolizes the grace of Spirit that nourishes us on our journey.

HEBREW LETTER: CHETH / FENCE
We can find our center only by using our Will to corral our emotions and mental chatter. The Chariot is a master of knowing when fences should be respected and when to jump the fence and head for the hills! Freedom requires building some fences from choice and removing or leaping over others that constrain us.

CHARIOT COLORING INSTRUCTIONS
White: Eagle, buildings (except rooftops), horse, charioteer's leggings.
Yellow: Mountains in the background.
Green: Trees, greenery, jewels on right horse's bridle and harness buckle.
Red: Rooftops, jewels on left horse's bridle and harness.
Orange: Wheels of chariot, streaks of energy.
Violet: Ribbons forming canopy and sides of chariot.
Silver: Moon and stars.
Brown: Tree trunks, horses' bridles, harnesses and reins, path.
Gold: Chalice, bits in horses' mouths, Charioteer's vest, sleeves, and leggings.
Gray: Chariot frame, wall before city, doorway, pillars.

Strength

Fierceness

I am the power of gentleness,
the heat of compassion,
the strength of kindness.
My art is to tame the beast
without whip, punishment, or fear.
My love blazes brightly,
conquering resistance,
embracing negativity,
neutralizing violence.
I skillfully bind
passion with presence,
anger with acceptance,
rejecting none,
using all wildness
as glorious fuel.

I am fiery Strength.

8 - Strength

OVERVIEW

The Strength card teaches us to embrace the difficult shadowy aspects of ourselves. Strength is not about overpowering that which we do not understand or which scares us, but learning to courageously work cooperatively with the energies of life. This is a beautiful internal move — to not use the power of the shadow against ourselves, but as a source of energy.

Pure acceptance and love is the most direct way to tame our internal demons. Anger, judgment, frustration, and fear only feed and empower the destructive elements. When we truly open our heart and move from peaceful stillness, we can befriend our fierceness. We learn to set clear boundaries with grace and dignity.

Strength reflects a robust conscious container that embraces all parts of self. We are each intimately linked to our desires and feelings, which we would do well not to ignore or battle. Working with, rather than against, our self grants us the energy to reveal hidden limitations and to heal old wounds.

When we acknowledge our own leonine demons, they stop scratching and biting us from the inside and begin to fuel our passion for creative change. This is the ultimate card of not taking anything personally, for looking past the right/wrong models, and for stepping into the fierceness of compassion, which exists beyond blame.

When you have a DEFICIENCY of the Strength energy, you probably
- Fear your inner animal and passion
- Live from a small and contracted place

When you have an EXCESS of Strength energy, you probably
- Force your way forward rather than move with what is
- Use your judge or your victim to control yourself or others with punishment and blame

SYMBOLS to help you dream the Strength card:

SUN RAYS
In the Toltec mythology, we are all rays of Light. The woman has embraced her individual ray of Light and so no longer sees any internal or external thing as a threat or a foe.

LION
The "King of the Jungle" represents our animal nature that can be destructive if untamed. The lion's claws and teeth are sheathed, yet the beast retains its sovereignty and power.

RIBBON
The spiraling ribbon shows how she has bound herself to her heart and integrity. She does not use chains to control or to dominate, but her ribbons create connection stemming from choice and sacred partnership.

INFINITY SIGN

This sacred symbol links her to the Magician. While his tools formed of Sky and Earth are external, her tools formed of heart and soul are internal. When we step into our true integrity, we open to infinity and all possibilities. The infinity symbol is also repeated in her dress.

ROSES

Blossoming from the Earth, roses represent desire and passion and how these qualities fuel growth.

HEBREW LETTER: TETH / SNAKE

The snake has long been a symbol of female power and of initiation. The snake teaches us the strength of fluidity and how to gain strength by letting go of old stories and limits.

STRENGTH COLORING INSTRUCTIONS

White: Woman's top dress, clouds.
Yellow: Eyes of lion, inside of skirt, sky background (with blue rays.)
Green: Rose leaves, skirt, shoe decorations, and bracelets.
Blue: Rays (light).
Red: Lion with brown highlights, roses, ribbon on wrist, infinity sign.
Brown: Sandals, foreground, highlights on lion.
Violet: Mountain in background, sky behind rays, highlights of clouds.

Hermit

9

The Hermit

Illumination

I am the gift of solitude,
of still mind and quiet hands,
deep breath and relaxed bones.
My art is to imbue all thoughts and acts with calm.
I eat the Light of solitude,
digest the universe,
drink the nothingness
until there are no more
ripples in the pond of self.
Alone I dissolve need, drama,
loneliness, doubt, fear,
until my flame burns brighter
than any darkness.
Now, I raise my lantern
and share this brilliance.

I am the shining Hermit.

9 - Hermit

OVERVIEW

The word hermit translates as "one of the desert." The Hermit ventures into the desert of his or her soul, consciously letting go of all attachments in order to drink from a deeper well. In the stillness, the Hermit begins not only to ponder, but also to embody wisdom. This is the wisdom that arises naturally when our attention is focused on our essence. The Hermit fills up with Truth and Light and then returns to his community to offer insight.

At times, we must journey to solitary places to aid our quest for wisdom. In the desert of the soul, everything we believe we are is stripped away and laid bare. The Hermit teaches us to move past all that we thought we were without fear. We learn to travel into the bare bones of our being and discover the indwelling wisdom that resides there.

The Hermit is alone, but not lonely. When we have not met our own soul, we can feel alone even if many loving friends and family members surround us. Once we pass through the initial loneliness of the desert, we discover a vastness of connection that is not dependent on people or external places. The Hermit holds the lantern high for others who are also seeking. This is not a mask or a strategy to be helpful or useful, but a gift offered without expectations. He has balanced and blended the masculine and feminine principles to become androgynous, beyond gender or identification. His emptiness is filled with wisdom that whispers from within every cell, muscle, bone, and organ.

When you have a DEFICIENCY of the Hermit energy, you probably
- Are afraid to be alone
- Rely on other people or distractions to feel comfortable

When you have an EXCESS of Hermit energy, you probably
- Isolate yourself to feel safe
- Do not share your gifts with others

SYMBOLS to help you dream the Hermit card:

LANTERN
The glowing lantern is a representation of the Hermit's inner Light, extended with love to provide Light for others and to spark their desire for liberation.

SIX-POINTED STAR
The shining star symbolizes the perfect balance of masculine and feminine blended together to create a single radiant force. The upward triangle represents the masculine (Sky), and the downward triangle represents the feminine (Earth.) The sacred union of these two powers is the catalyst for awakening to universal wisdom.

STAFF
The supportive staff reflects that inner wisdom comes from maturity and walking life's path of varied experiences. It shows that the Hermit leans on the strength of God/dess and that he also serves as a shepherd for his people.

Hermit

FOOT
The Hermit steps forward towards the world with his left foot. Guided by his intuition while fully utilizing his senses, he follows the path that will lead him to those who seek the Light.

HEBREW LETTER: YOD / OPEN HAND
Yod is a messenger or guide connecting Spirit to the physical realm. It depicts an open, creative, or helping hand. The yod rests on the hermit's head, showing that he is sheltered and nourished by a greater supportive force.

HERMIT COLORING INSTRUCTIONS
White: Hair, sleeves, snow on mountains, inner garment at chest.
Yellow: Rays around star, inside of hood, staff.
Blue: Yod on head, decorations on lantern, brooch on chest.
Gray: Robe, sides of peak the Hermit stands upon, lighter gray for inside trim of sleeves and bottom edge of robe, mountains.
Violet: Sky behind rays (dark indigo color).
Brown: Shoe.
Silver: Lantern.
Gold: Star inside lantern.

10

Wheel of Fortune

Turning

I am the churning power of life,
the unstoppable cycles
of birth, death, rebirth.
My art is the splendor of constant change.
I am beyond all control
and manipulation.
I defy logic.
One second, I seem cruel –
the next second, a blessing.
I am neither.
No one is favored or exempt
from my motion.
Will you feel crushed beneath me,
or laugh at the beauty
of the uncontrollable?

I am the spinning Wheel of Fortune.

10- Wheel of Fortune

OVERVIEW

The Wheel of Fortune moves in cycles. How do we respond to these cycles and spirals of life? Are we caught in the spokes or have we learned to witness and enjoy the turning of the Wheel? At times it feels that life is running over us; other times, it feels as if we are directing the Wheel. In either case, the wheel is beyond our control.

There may be times when we feel "complete" or centered in our own process, only to fall into a place of judgment and fear in response to a tiny event. Or, we may be submerged in our own pain and suddenly feel the heavens open to us. In either case, when we learn not to grasp at what is in front of us, we welcome both the up and the down.

When we fall into illusion around life's Wheel, we suffer. We cannot control the Wheel, but we can learn to rise above it and to watch the beauty of its motion as the Sphinx has done. The Wheel contains all of life: the hellos and the goodbyes, the joys and the pains, the births and the deaths. We may cringe from some of its aspects and grasp at others, yet all are simply part of its ceaseless flow.

When we clutch, we soon spin off center, swept into the drama. As we let go of taking life personally or wanting it to be pleasant or understandable or controllable, we rise above our changing circumstances to witness the larger patterns and cycles. The Wheel teaches us to honor change and the reversal of fortune.

When you have a DEFICIENCY of the Wheel of Fortune energy, you probably
- Feel crushed by the weight of life
- Hold the illusion that you can control the outcome of all things

When you have an EXCESS of Wheel of Fortune energy, you probably
- Never allow yourself to feel stable
- Feel alive only when big changes are happening

SYMBOLS to help you dream the Wheel of Fortune card:

SYMBOLS
Within the wheel are the alchemical symbols that represent change (mercury, sulfur, salt, and water). The letters spell out "Rota" (wheel), "Tora" (knowledge), "Orat" (oracle), and "Tarot" (secret or mystery).

SNAKE
This mythic creature is a symbol of our expansion and the concomitant shedding of our skin during each cycle of growth.

SPHINX AND ANUBIS
The Sphinx is the gatekeeper of Truth who rides above the wheel. Anubis holds the wheel and serves as the soul's guide to the underworld. We are supported even at our darkest moments.

Wheel of Fortune

OUTER FIGURES

The four images represent the four fixed signs of the zodiac: Bull for Taurus, Lion for Leo, Eagle for Scorpio, and Human for Aquarius. They demonstrate how a firm foundation stabilizes you from the spinning of the Wheel of Fortune. These four figures also represent the four archangels.

HEBREW LETTER: KAPH / HAND

Spirit grasps our fate and the Wheel. We can struggle and grasp or we can remember that we are lovingly held in the hands of the Divine.

WHEEL OF FORTUNE COLORING INSTRUCTIONS

White: Circles around four outer figures, bull's horns, eye, skirt, and headdress of Anubis and the Sphinx.
Yellow: Serpent, eagle's eye and beak, lion's eye.
Blue: Sky (with swirls of gray), Sphinx (darker blue), background of four outer figures.
Red: Anubis.
Orange: Wheel edges, with inner design a darker orange.
Brown: Animals with lion tawny (brown mixed with yellow).
Gray: Sword (dark gray), swirls in sky (except centers).
Gold: Sword handle, letters and symbols in wheel.

Justice

11

Justice

Balance

I am the ever present Witness
of all actions, thoughts,
and deeds.
My art is the dance of cause and effect.
I hold the scales that weigh every nuance,
not to punish
or to bring guilt,
but to teach
the creed of impeccability:
All things return.
Heaviness begets heaviness;
Lightness begets lightness.
Beneath the seen is
a deeper weaving.
Are you witnessing?

I am pure Justice.

11 ~ Justice

OVERVIEW

Justice teaches us to move beyond our limited ideas of good and evil to a greater faith in the workings of the Universe. From childhood, we are trained that justice invokes punishment of bad actions and reward of good actions. This works on the surface, yet does not lead to greater self-awareness and self-responsibility.

The old punishment matrix uses judgment, guilt, and shame to keep us in line. A reward is an external pacifier such as acceptance or conditional love. We often will do whatever is necessary to earn the reward, even if it violates our own integrity. When we grasp for reward or flee from punishment, we are off-center and inauthentic.

Whatever thoughts and beliefs we adopted in childhood cycle back to affect our lives today. When we act to heal and clear out the old masks from the past and face our fears, we positively shape our future. This card represents the principle of action and reaction — what we put into the world comes back to us.

Many things lie beyond our control, and we must learn to surrender to a higher Source. When we embody Justice energy, we accept our role in bringing justice into the world where we can and trusting that Spirit will take care of the rest. Determine what really lies in your sphere of influence and release what is not.

The Toltec Tarot

When you have a DEFICIENCY of Justice energy, you probably
- Feel that life is not fair
- Believe that everyone else is responsible for your actions and feelings

When you have an EXCESS of Justice energy, you probably
- Believe that you know what is right for people (self-righteousness)
- Feel you have to take situations or causes into your own hands to make them fair/just

SYMBOLS to help you dream the Justice card:

PILLARS
The figure sits between pillars, as do the High Priestess and the Hierophant. Justice is a bridge between the Spirit world and the human world. The curtains represent the hidden spiritual realms where true justice originates.

SCALE
Mind and heart are balanced. There is no judgment, simply what is. All actions are weighed equally. Heavy energy will create more heavy energy; light energy will create more light energy.

SWORD
Discerning intuition incorporates mind and heart as it cuts to Truth like a sword.

FOOT
The foot is extended, ready to act.

SYMBOL ON CHEST
Justice wears a T on her chest that links her to the Empress. Both she and the Empress feel deeply and hold themselves steadily, knowing that they do not need to act on all of their feelings.

HEBREW LETTER: LAMED / OX-GOAD
The prod is a means to nudge someone to stay on their path and to educate them. Justice is the way that the universe instructs us to make more supportive choices in our life.

JUSTICE COLORING INSTRUCTIONS
White: Around center of tiara, area under and just below T on chest, floor.
Yellow: Stars in the background.
Dark blue: Main part of armbands (trimmed with violet).
Green: Cape (just over her shoulders), anklet.
Red: Robe, tassels, circle in emblem on tiara, bindi on forehead.
Violet: Curtains, oval and T around neck, veil connecting pillars (a lighter shade), trim of bracelets.
Gray: Pillars (except top), blade of sword (darker gray), floor.
Gold: Scale, sword hilt, top of pillars, outer tiara.

Hanged One

12

Hanged One

Reversal

I am beyond the mind's grasp –
up becomes down;
down becomes up.
My art is to turn everything upside-down
and look again,
and look again.
I smile as I understand Truth:
what is opposite of right
is not wrong.
I sacrifice the known, the safe,
the understood
for something greater.
I am a drop of rain
dissolving into
the all-knowing sea.

I am the fluid Hanged One.

12 - Hanged One

OVERVIEW

The Hanged One speaks to us of the power of sacrifice. Sacrifice occurs when we renounce something of value to make space for something of greater value to enter our lives. We may sacrifice the pleasure of eating sugar for a healthier body, or we may need to sacrifice our need to be right (or in control, or perfect...) all the time for being happy and centered in ourselves.

The Hanged One is not the sacrifice of the martyr or victim, but the well-chosen self-sacrifice of the warrior. This offering is made consciously to attain what is best in the long run.

With his hands tied behind his back, the Hanged One chooses to relinquish personal control. He understands that once he has acted from his integrity, he must then completely let go of the outcome. This inspired action allows the Hanged One to access a higher voice and a higher wisdom. He teaches us to regularly turn our lives and our perspective upside-down. His mantras are "I do not know" and "Let's see!"

The Hanged One represents the importance of learning to surrender gracefully. We release control of what we know about ourselves or others and the need to be right. We let go of taking responsibility for others' emotional responses or fears. Ah, what a relief!

The Toltec Tarot

When you have a DEFICIENCY of Hanged One energy, you probably
- Struggle against change and loss
- Refuse to let go of your perspective

When you have an EXCESS of Hanged One energy, you probably
- Surrender your Will as a protection to keep yourself liked or safe
- Believe that sacrificing everything will win you love and acceptance

SYMBOLS to help you dream the Hanged One card:

FEET OVER HEAD
This reversal of normal orientation positions the head/mind in the roots of the Tree of Life and the feet/root in the sky.

JACKET
The moons and four buttons on the lower jacket invoke the High Priestess and Emperor. This balance of Earth energy and moon energy leads to psychic stability.

COAT
The six buttons on top of coat correspond to the number of the Lovers card. When we surrender completely, our inner marriage is deepened, opening new vistas and worlds.

Hanged One

LEGS

The position of the Hanged One's legs creates the numeral 4, which echoes the Emperor again. By reversing our perspective, we create new stability by viewing our structure with new eyes.

PYRAMID

The Pyramid of the Sun of Teotihuacán is the final destination for the Hanged One's journey of surrender. This card shows the start of the journey and its potential for completion.

HEBREW LETTER: MEM / WATER

Mem points to the power of self-reflection that arises when we release our assumptions and expectations before peering into the mirror of our lives. We achieve a new sense of flow and ease by dissolving those places where we need to know or need to be perfect.

HANGED ONE COLORING INSTRUCTIONS

White: Rope, inner sun.
Yellow: Shoes, halo around head, flower in grass, sunrays.
Blue: Jacket (except ornaments).
Red: Hose, fruit in tree, tattoo.
Green: Grass, leaves.
Orange: Pyramid.
Brown: Tree trunks, slopes of earth.
Gray: Sky between rays.
Silver: Belt, buttons, pockets, and jacket edgings.

13

Death

The Toltec Tarot

Dissolution

I am the final sword of Truth
ending hope and desire,
cutting all ties.
My art is compassionate severing
of ego, of structure, of form –
Wipe the slate clean and start again.
All things pass through my arms –
from rock to flesh,
thoughts to civilizations –
and become no more.
I have patience. No one
evades me. Will you choose to fear
or trust my embrace?
This you control.
All else belongs to me.

I am the Angel of Death.

13 - Death

OVERVIEW

The Death card represents many different types of death — the death of the body, the death of the ego, the death of old belief systems and structures. Death is a crucial and beneficial part of the cycle in order for new life and growth to flourish. It clears the fields of life, so the old will not impede the new. New life literally feeds on death.

When you release an agreement or allow an old image of yourself to die, you liberate energy necessary to create a new agreement and new ways of being. Death gifts us with energy, space, and resources. We do not need to fear it, but to learn to embrace all of its aspects. This card depicts both early morning and twilight, for in Death, there is always a beginning and an ending.

In the Kaballah teachings, death actually occurs when we are first born because we are dying to the Spirit world to assume form. When we die physically, we are birthed back into Spirit. That is how the Hanged One views death – very differently than our usual interpretation!

We are all going to die physically. When we embrace rather than resist the Angel of Death, she teaches us how to truly live. As don Miguel once said, "Most people are not really afraid to die; they are afraid to live." By acting as if the Angel of Death walked just behind you, you learn to fully live your life in the present moment, with complete awareness and gratitude.

The Toltec Tarot

When you have a DEFICIENCY of Death energy, you probably
- Have a lot of clutter in your life, both physically and emotionally
- Fear loss

When you have an EXCESS of Death energy, you probably
- Do not see the worth of living and yearn for release
- Feel the weight of loss all around you

SYMBOLS to help you dream the Death card:

BUBBLES AND BONES
The figures in the bubbles and the bones show how death has no mercy--it indiscriminately takes the young and old, male and female, impoverished and royalty.

SCYTHE
Death harvests life to provide space for new growth.

BRIDGE
The span represents the place of no return. Once we cross the bridge to face the Angel of Death, all that we know will be extinguished by her embrace.

ROSES
At death, all things are returned to their pure essence.

PYRAMID
The Pyramid of the Moon calls us forward and invites us

to let go, knowing that the Mystery will rebirth us.

HEBREW LETTER: NUN / FISH
Fish represent abundance and vibrancy in spiritual life. The fish reminds us to have faith and to look beyond physical death, knowing that we will live on in a new form.

DEATH COLORING INSTRUCTIONS
White: Angel of Death skeleton, bones, roses, inner energy rising from pyramid, highlights of mountains, stars, bubble interiors, walkway to pyramid, stars inside Death's "face."
Blue: River, bubble exteriors.
Green: Rosebush leaves.
Red: Sky, Death's robe, point on scythe.
Violet: Trim of Death's robe, belt, and jewel at throat.
Brown: Land on either side of the walkway (light brown), handle of scythe.
Gray: Mountains, bridge walls, blade of scythe (dark gray), pyramid, plaza, rocks.
Silver: Outer edges of energy rising from pyramid, energy around Death.
Gold: Crown on man's head.

Temperance

14

Temperance

Butterfly

I am the blessing of harmony,
a whisper of love,
the echo of infinity embodied.
My art is reconciliation
of the inner fire's
passion, anger, and fierce joy
with the watery depths'
acceptance, grief, and spontaneous bliss.
I use all struggles and sweetness
as purification.
I hold the alchemy of fire and water
as I let them flow into Earth
with Sky as my witness.
Birth yourself from the space
between the atoms.

I am radiant Temperance.

14 - Temperance

OVERVIEW

In Temperance, we surrender to the flames of purification, transforming with an open heart and a non-judging mind. Here, self-consciousness and the subconscious work in harmony to blend and balance fire and water. This unification calls forth the best in both elements. We dance in the middle, soothing the fire with cooling water while stimulating the water with fiery energy.

When steel is tempered, heat and pressure are used to strengthen the metal. Similarly, when a butterfly emerges from its cocoon, it must struggle in order to strengthen its wings. If someone prematurely frees the butterfly from its cocoon, it will not be able to fly because its crucial tempering stage was omitted.

If we shirk the hard work of breaking down our old confining structures or if our freedom is conditional on other people, we will not have developed what is required to truly inhabit our essential nature. In contrast, love will open our wings when we stand in our own center.

The Temperance card is also known as the consummation or the alchemical marriage. The opposite parts of our self are reconciled as we embrace both Lover and Devil energies. We create a larger living space for ourselves by utilizing all our previous experiences to create harmony, even within chaos.

When you have a DEFICIENCY of Temperance energy, you probably
- Cyclically struggle without benefit
- Swing erratically between fire and water energies

When you have an EXCESS of Temperance energy, you probably
- Believe the struggle is the outcome
- Fixedly hold on to power and strength

SYMBOLS to help you dream the Temperance card:

VASES
Temperance shows her mastery of the elements by containing them in vases. Our power lies in first containing our passions and emotions and then allowing them to flow back to Source.

RAINBOW FEATHERS
The feather headdress signifies her connection to Sky and her freedom. The feathers are arrayed in a rainbow pattern, a symbol of the transformational process.

FOOT
Temperance steps into the mysterious depth of water while the other foot remains on solid earth.

TEMPLE SPACE
By containing her fire and water, Temperance creates herself as sacred space, honoring her being as a temple.

Temperance

BUTTERFLIES

The three butterflies represent the trinity — opposites reconciled into a new third being.

HEBREW LETTER: SAMEKH / FOUNDATION

This letter signifies that Temperance blossoms from the support of a higher power. The foundation is created from balancing opposite forces.

TEMPERANCE COLORING INSTRUCTIONS

White: Clouds, inside of necklace, loincloth, bracelets, belt, design on vases.

Yellow: Flames.

Red: Angel's wings (with blue inside and violet edges), inner flames.

Blue: Stream from vase, ripples from hole, inside of wings, floor (light blue).

Orange: Vases (except for white designs), headdress, walls and outer edge of wall designs (gold on inner designs).

Violet: Outer edge of wings, smaller butterflies (with red highlights).

Gold: Background sky, all body decorations, earrings, inner designs on walls.

Rainbow: Violet center feather, with feathers fanning out from center in this order: blue, green, yellow, orange, and red.

Devil

Adversary

I am the voice of fear,
the whisper of betrayal,
the cry of abandonment.
My art is weaving illusion,
wrapping stories to trap
awareness and wisdom.
Trust me.
There is not enough.
You are not enough.
You are weak, flawed, trapped.
And as you believe me, I eat well.
Fear is my bread,
confusion my dessert.
And though I appear the enemy
I could be your greatest ally.

I am the tempting Devil.

15 - The Devil

OVERVIEW

The Devil card includes the mirror image of the Lovers — a union based in fear and scarcity. It depicts the outcome of trying to overcome our sense of separateness through addictions and bondage to unhealthy beliefs and patterns. The Devil is also an Angel, but he is an Angel that feeds on fear. Like all Angels, he is a gift from Spirit to bring us back to wholeness.

The Devil card teaches us how to use our addictions to guide us to Truth. We are all addicted to something, whether it be a physical substance or a pattern of thought. All addictions stem from a false sense of separation, including drinking, gossiping, drugging, feeling victimized, thinking too much, and feeding off drama and chaos. We can use our current dramas and pain to keep us cycling in Hell. Or we can use them to pinpoint where we need to clear out the shackles of old emotions and beliefs within our energy system.

The saying "What does not kill you will make you stronger" hints at the importance of the Devil card in our lives. As plainly seen in the card, the chains around the two humans' necks are loose. While our bondage to fear and self-sabotage may seem impenetrable, with awareness we realize that the path to freedom is within our reach. All the stories are illusions. Every adversary, internal or external, is a gift to help you track and to clean out those hidden agreements.

The Toltec Tarot

When you have a DEFICIENCY of Devil energy, you probably
- Are depressed and have given up all hope because the Devil is hiding inside
- Pretend that you are a saint or a martyr

When you have an EXCESS of Devil energy, you probably
- Have a strongly addictive or controlling personality
- Imagine evil and darkness in situations and people

SYMBOLS to help you dream the Devil card:

HEADS
Cut off from their bodies, the heads try and think their way to freedom, only to become more confused and muddled. Confusion is one of the Devil's most effective tools.

DEVIL
This figure is a representation of the Archangel Uriel, who is called the Light of God.

CHAINS
The chain connects us to the Will of the Devil instead of the Will of the Divine. This connection is pure illusion; the chains appear solid even though they are already broken.

HAND GESTURE, GLYPHS
His hand is raised in a gesture of "brotherhood." When

we connect to the Devil, we assume the fears of those around us. The glyph for Saturn in the flame reflects his control of your inner fire. The stylized glyph for Mercury represents the Devil's twisting of communication to keep you believing his voice, rather than your own Truth.

SHELLS AND DOORWAY

These symbols come from Teotihuacán's "portal," an underground temple. The shells represent the importance of fluidity, and the portal allows one to travel wherever they wish. To step through the portal, you must be able to move beyond your own fears and insecurities, past any inner Devils that block the path.

HEBREW LETTER: AYIN / HUMAN EYE

This Hebrew letter represents an open eye, which can see beyond illusions. The Devil watches and rules over us or we can watch the Devil and ascertain his hidden motives.

DEVIL COLORING INSTRUCTIONS

White: Stars in background, wall in background.
Yellow: Symbol on chest, flames (streaked with red), halo.
Green: Shells.
Red: Highlights in flames, main body of wings, star on forehead, horns.
Brown: Torch handle, Devil's body, wing veins (all grayed brown), cloth and all jewelry (dark brown).
Gray: Portal, chains (dark gray).

Tower

16

The Tower

Lightning

I am the irreconcilable
end of form, the hand of God
severing the old.
My art is the necessary destruction
of all outdated structures.
My brilliance shatters
egos, relationships, families, worlds,
so the pieces no longer fit,
no matter how you try to regress.
It is done. Weep at the rubble.
Release the crumbled shell.
Now dance.
Celebrate the new beginning
that comes with each and every
ending.

I am the transformative Tower.

16 - The Tower

OVERVIEW

Tower energy flashes through our lives like lightning, destroying what no longer serves us. This is not a subtle card, rather an undeniable crumbling of our structure that often shelters our sense of safety. We are ejected from the known and hurled into the unknown to create a new way of Living. This card follows the Devil card, and it clearly demonstrates what can happen if we ignore our addictions and denials. The Tower energy is fierce and ruthless, and when the smoke clears and we pick ourselves back up, we find that we must start over.

The Tower card powerfully helps us to balance our mental, physical, and emotional bodies. A drastic correction is required when we continue to repress emotions, fabricate stories not based in Truth, or ignore our bodies. Our "towers" are emotional, mental, or physical constructs based in unconscious actions and agreements. The Divine shines a bright Light that illuminates and penetrates through to our rocky foundation.

Continue to surrender to the fact that you are not in control. There are many external forces that can create sudden change! Will you allow the tower of your ego to crumble? Will you surrender to the end of the relationship, job, or self-image? Refusing to release the rubble of the tower can cause tremendous suffering. The Tower reminds us to face our fears without delay, so we can stabilize and mature from the firm foundations of love.

When you have a DEFICIENCY of Tower energy, you probably
- Stay far away from any edges in your life
- Reject change and flow for safety and predictability

When you have an EXCESS of Tower energy, you probably
- Feel most alive when you are enmeshed in high drama
- Have an unconscious pattern of choosing high risk/unstable situations

SYMBOLS to help you dream the Tower card:

TOWER IMAGERY
This gripping portrayal dates back to the Tower of Babel, which humans built in order to challenge God. God struck down the tower, and from thence forth, humans spoke (babbled) in different languages.

PERSON FALLING
The person falling represents too much ego, too much emotional drama, and too much desire. Like Death, Tower energy affects everyone – young and old, rich and poor.

LIGHTNING AND CLOUDS
Clouds and lightning show it is Spirit that steps in to restore balance by destroying what is not Truth. This action bestows the gifts of humility and acceptance.

MOON
The Tower's destruction often unmasks deeply buried emotions and subconscious motives.

HEBREW LETTER: PEI / MOUTH
The destruction of our Tower is caused by all the places where we are not impeccable with our word. Our lies to self and others will eventually lead to drama and chaos.

TOWER COLORING INSTRUCTIONS
White: Edges of clouds, energy of man falling, lightning, energy around tower.
Yellow: Top of tower (decorations are gold), highlights of streaks coming from tower.
Blue: Man's shirt and skirt (all decorations on clothing is red.)
Red: Decorations on man's clothing, including bracelets and shoes, lines and streaks coming from tower (red with yellow highlights except streaks from falling man).
Brown: Mountains (with darker brown-gray veins), sandals.
Gray: Storm clouds, clouds over mountains (gray with white edges), Tower.
Gold: Decorations and small squares on top of Tower.

Star

17

The Star

Nourishment

I am the softness of
sweet reflection.
My art is cultivating cellular peace –
opening each cell to
drink deeply
from the waters
of communion.
Look at your
true reflection.
You are already whole.
You are perfect.
You radiate as a
pinpoint of Light.
Fill yourself at the well
of your own beauty.

I am the healing Star.

17 - The Star

OVERVIEW

The Star card follows the Tower's destruction of illusion. We discover peace and inner harmony, a quiet sense of relaxation. Our struggles end when we surrender our need to control and simply accept ourselves unconditionally.

This card teaches us how to deeply nourish and to love ourselves. We rest in the abundance of energy and the supporting allies that surround us. From this place, we instinctively become a channel of Light and communication between Earth and Sky. We remember that we are each a unique Light in the world, and we are no longer afraid to let our brilliance shine.

When we reclaim our own star, we allow the Divine to work through us. Instead of struggling or forcing an outcome, we patiently listen with all of our senses open for our next step on the journey to reveal itself. The sparkling waters of life flow through us, and we luxuriate in their nurturing embrace. The Star card reminds us of the importance of releasing tension and worry while relaxing into the healing that envelopes us.

Similar to snowflakes, there are no two stars that are exactly alike. Set an intent to align with your energetic center, and stop comparing yourself to others or wishing that things were somehow different. Rest in the beauty of your being, and allow your life to become a reflection of your own divine star.

When you have a DEFICIENCY of Star energy, you probably
- Do not create time to nourish yourself
- Hide your inner Light under layers of shame or protection

When you have an EXCESS of Star energy, you probably
- Are narcissistic
- Use body image as a distraction or a way to stay passive

SYMBOLS to help you dream the Star card:

STAR
The celestial star represents your connection to Spirit. When we align ourselves with Spirit, we become a star. The smaller stars represent each of the seven chakras.

NAKEDNESS
The Star has dropped all veils and illusions to be in this present moment, unburdened and unafraid.

WATER
The Star pours water from one vase into the self-reflecting water. The subsequent ripples show how our being shimmers out from our Center. The other vase pours water onto the earth, to nourish it. Water always returns to its source just as we will return to our Source of pure awareness and love. The star within links us to this greater energy.

IBIS

The sacred ibis reflects the grace and calm that descend when we step into our center.

HEBREW LETTER: TZADDI / FISHHOOK

We fish in the sacred waters for inspiration and wisdom. The hook of our integrity summons heaven's Light.

STAR COLORING INSTRUCTIONS

White: Seven smaller stars, middle of large star, highlights on water, edges of clouds.

Yellow: Outer energy around star, rays emanating from star, large ray around figure (edged in gold).

Blue: Sky, clouds, water in pool and pouring from vases, bottom strip and top half of triangles of vases (other half is red, so they alternate).

Green: Foliage.

Red: Bird, top strip and half of triangle on vases (other half blue).

Orange: Vases (except decorations).

Brown: Sandy area on shore (light brown), rocks around water (darker brown).

Gold: Middle star (center one white), two rays coming down on either side of figure.

18

The Moon

Depth

I am the innate understanding,
the hidden
biological knowing.
My art is diving the ocean of instinct,
activating the hidden gateway
of intuition.
All feel my pull
of tide and blood and emotions.
I am the primordial waters flowing through
the collective unconscious,
from animal to human to Divine.
Dive in. Melt
into the buoyant embrace
of the universal
womb.

I am the instinctual Moon.

18 - The Moon

OVERVIEW

The Moon's ever changing face resonates with the dance of the Earth around the sun and the natural cycles of life. We are all enmeshed in an evolutionary process, moving from our animal selves through the human to connect with the Divine. The Moon reminds us of the many fluid ways to weave our total being together. We swim in the waters of the moonlight, knowing that everything changes, even as it stays the same. From this place of fearless compassion, we serve the greater good from a deep love for self as a reflection of Spirit.

On this journey, we do not cut ourselves off from our Source. We are animals. We are creatures of nature. Our wild intuitive selves connect us to vast reservoirs of energy and information. We all emerged from the womb of creation and are linked by our common Source. We can tap the fears and unresolved issues that hide in the watery unconscious or we can connect to the deep wisdom of wildness, acting from our passion and instinct. The Moon's gift is the innate wisdom of the body with its incredible sensitivity and capacity for healing.

Our power and creativity lie beneath our addictions and fear. The Moon calls us to dive into the unknown and to learn to swim. In this place, we discover the lessons of our ancestors. We find the dream of humanity, the full emotional range, and the collective unconscious. Learn to notice the shining threads of wisdom reflected by the Moon in the most unexpected places.

When you have a DEFICIENCY of Moon energy, you probably
- Have cut yourself off from your intuition
- Allow the rational mind and scientific fact to guide you

When you have an EXCESS of Moon energy, you probably
- Feel that you will drown in your unconscious fears
- Lean on ANY impulse or desire that arises to guide you

SYMBOLS to help you dream the Moon card:

DOG/WOLF
The integration of wild self and domesticated self is symbolized by the transformation of unconscious, untamed desires (wolf) into conscious, tamed thoughts (dog). This movement transports us beyond ego and into the unity of all beings.

CRAWFISH
The crawfish reminds us of our primordial connection back to the womb of the ocean. It hints of our evolution towards Earth and then into the Divine.

PYRAMID
The Pyramid of the Moon in Teotihuacán is positioned at the end of the Avenue of the Dead. It is a sacred place of connection with the Divine Mother and emanates a sweet shimmering energy.

HEBREW LETTER: QOPH / BACK OF THE HEAD
The back of the head points to hidden messages and the area of the reptilian brain stem (seat of reflexive thought, heartbeat, breath, etc.) This area of our brain relates to instinct and our receptivity to the sacred.

MOON COLORING INSTRUCTIONS

White: Ruff on the wolf, Moon, outer energy around Moon and rays (with silver inside), large inverted chalice on top of Moon.

Blue: Stairs on pyramid, outer steps flanking the Pyramid of the Moon, edge of platform.

Green: Grass in foreground.

Violet: Crawfish, platform dogs sit upon.

Brown: Dog on right (light brown).

Silver: Pyramid of the Moon highlights, energy coming off pyramid, Moon, rays from Moon (with inner white streak).

Gray: Pyramid of the Moon (with silver highlights), wolf on left.

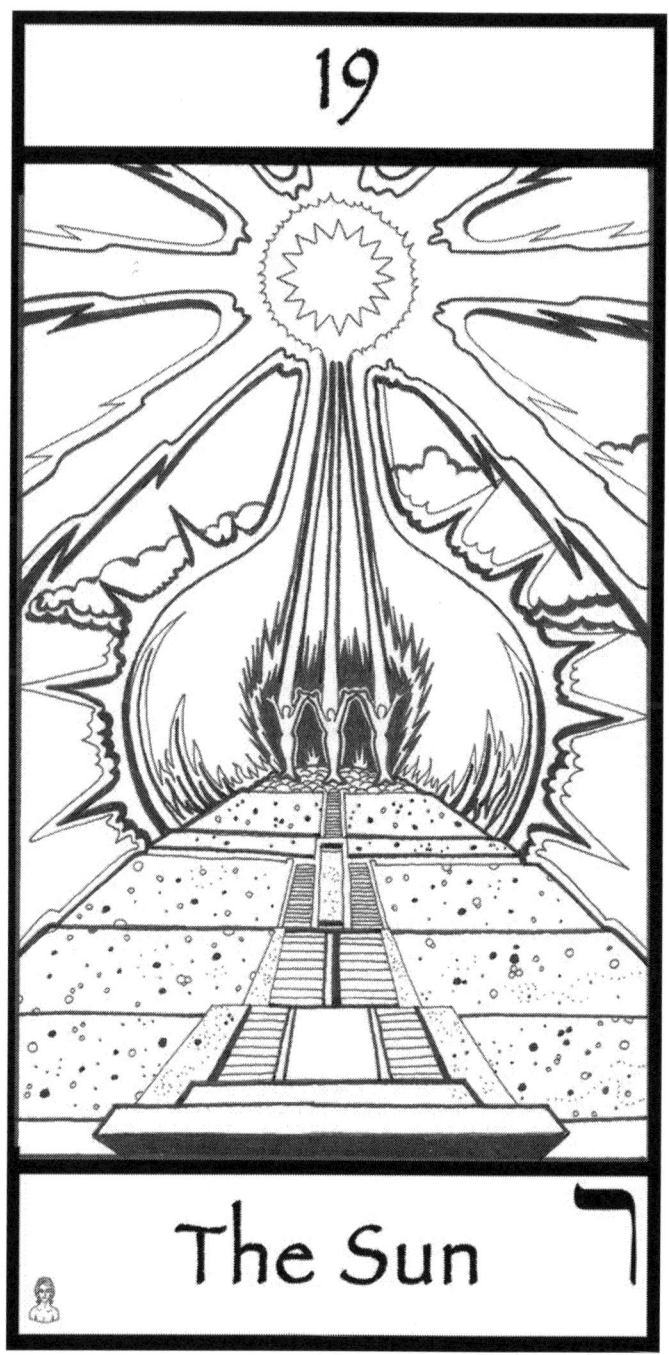

Sun

19

The Sun

Shine

I am the ecstasy
of matter becoming
unfettered love.
My art is full blossoming,
complete expansion of human
to Divine.
You are not flesh and bone
but a ray of sunshine,
a column of energy,
laughing liquid Light.
Stop holding back.
Your brilliance is
a gift, a prayer,
a fulfilled promise
from God.

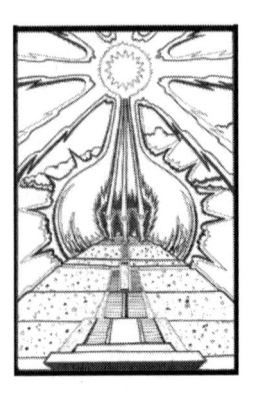

I am the shining Sun.

19 - The Sun

OVERVIEW

The Sun card teaches us about the power of pure joy and celebration of life. Our energy can flow into pure exuberant play when there are no masks to maintain and no need to act a certain way. When we fully connect to the Light of the Sun shining upon us, our hearts open and we see the positive aspects of life reflected in all things. We direct our own experiences with the reins of a positive well-balanced mind. Tasks that used to be tedious chores become effortless, even fun!

A Hafiz poem illustrates the unconditional nature of Sun energy: Even after all these years / The sun never says to the earth / You owe me. / Imagine a love like that. / It lights the whole sky.

When we share ourselves in service to the Divine, we do not expect anything in return. Yet the whole sky is lit by our actions. A life of unconditional service, love, and celebration elicits the best in our community and ourselves. We glow with life, shining pure potential around us. Our actions arise not from denial or repression, but from a desire to gratefully see the Divine in all.

The Sun card is the natural outcome of clearing fear and self-doubt from our being. When we untangle our agreements and find our own integrity, we become like children again: Curious fiery beings who find wonder and magic in all things.

The Toltec Tarot

When you have a DEFICIENCY of Sun energy, you probably
- Are afraid to share your Light
- See the world as a serious place of suffering and responsibility

When you have an EXCESS of Sun energy, you probably
- Have taken on a mask of merriment and humor to hide your sadness
- Have merged with God so thoroughly that you neglect your physical form

SYMBOLS to help you dream the Sun card:

SUN
The Sun shines as the living reflection of the true self, just as the Moon is a reflection of the emotional self.

FIGURES
The upright forms represent your pure child-like essence and the joy of sacred community coming together to celebrate and honor life.

PYRAMID
The Sun card is connected to Christ consciousness and unconditional love.

HEBREW LETTER: RESH / FACE
The human face and head is an expression of revealing oneself without masks. This symbol also relates to the

Sun

crown chakra and our ability to access a higher consciousness.

SUN COLORING INSTRUCTIONS

White: Clouds in sky, outside edge of energy surrounding the Sun, the streaks of energy within the inverted chalice above the figures.

Yellow: Inner Sun, large rays extending out from the Sun, figures on the solar energy around and between rays (gold) shining down on figures.

Red: Pyramid rocks and staircases.

Blue: Sky.

Green: Very bottom platform and edge of pyramid.

Orange: Pyramid, with red rocks and staircases.

Violet: Edges of clouds.

Gold: Ring around the Sun and rays extending down to people, edges of large rays.

20

Judgment

Awakening

I am the end of
self-punishment and abuse.
My art is unconditional witnessing.
Wake up.
This mind chatter is not who you are.
You are not that charming personality
or important identity.
No boxes can define you.
No words can hurt you.
Sheathe the sharp blade
of your word and cease stabbing
your precious self.
May this moment be the
birth of total
self-forgiveness.

I am the final Judgment.

20 - Judgment

OVERVIEW

The Judgment card illustrates three people rising from boxes, representing their ego, structure, and agreements. All aspects of ourselves are reflected in this card. We are the Angels, beckoning those sleeping parts of ourselves to awaken. We are the figures rising and facing the Light. We are the limitations of the boxes, and we are the limitless ocean. When we accept our shadow and our Light equally and without judgment, we rebirth ourselves.

This is the final Judgment, not ordained by an outside source, but arising from our own Intent to stop judging others and ourselves. This card evokes inner reflection, alignment with wisdom, and integration beyond any external or internal judge. The trumpet is our wake-up call to step out of our boxes and to learn new ways of being in the world.

What lies beyond the judge? The Judgment card stretches us beyond our ego and self-limiting beliefs, beyond this lifetime into the timelessness of multi-dimensional living. When we fully embody this card, we understand on a cellular level that there is nothing to judge in others and ourselves. We are on a journey of growth. All mistakes and painful experiences can be used to facilitate that growth, rather than to make ourselves wrong. We learn to witness ourselves and all others through the eyes of the Angel, through the eyes of the Divine.

The Toltec Tarot

When you have a DEFICIENCY of Judgment energy, you probably
- Are waiting for an outside force to forgive you for your sins
- Do not discern between what supports you and what sabotages you

When you have an EXCESS of Judgment energy, you probably
- Use your judge to motivate you to act
- Are trapped in your ego and need others to be wrong so you can be right

SYMBOLS to help you dream the Judgment card:

ANGEL
The Archangel Gabriel is the messenger of God/Goddess.

TRUMPET
Musical messages resonate on a vibratory level, to awaken our God/dess-self.

FLAG
The circular flag on Gabriel's trumpet is a reminder that when we integrate the four elements of self (mental, spiritual, emotional, and physical), we find our center.

NAKEDNESS
The figures' nudity is a representation of freedom. They arise exactly as they are, unashamed to stand naked before each other and the Divine.

OCEAN

The stream of the High Priestess has become the ocean, which signifies completion.

HEBREW LETTER: SHIN / TOOTH

Judgment appears after we thoroughly "chew" and assimilate our experiences, which leads to wisdom.

JUDGMENT COLORING INSTRUCTIONS

White: Clouds, interior of circular flag, angle's sleeve and robe trim on Angel
Yellow: Rays from trumpet and Angel.
Blue: Sky, water (with white highlights), Angel's robe (darker blue).
Red: Interior design of banner, Angel's wings (mixed with violet).
Violet: Angel's wings (mixed with red), mountains in background (highlighted with white).
Gray: Human bodies, coffins (darker gray).
Gold: Trumpet exterior.
Rainbow colors: Fourteen rays from trumpet from left to right: red, orange, yellow, green, blue, indigo, violet and then repeat red through violet.

Cosmos

Completion

I am whole,
seamlessly woven into
the tapestry of life.
My art is complete freedom –
perfect choice,
perfect trust.
I dance myself
wide open,
every atom,
until the world weaves into me
and I melt into the world.
No more striving,
I have arrived.
One word echoes within me:
Yes.

I am the vibrant Cosmos.

21-Cosmos

OVERVIEW

In the Cosmos card, we see the final integration of all of life's lessons, not as a mental construct, but a deeply felt knowing. Here the individual has completely mastered the workings of the Tarot. The central figure is androgynous, holding the perfect balance of male and female, Earth and Sky. The figure balances on one foot, dancing on air while supported by the universe. When we integrate all of our tools, we no longer need a structure to hold us, for our faith uplifts us.

Integrity is achieved when we honor and respect all parts of our self as Divine. By assimilating the tools and lessons of each of the Tarot cards, we embrace an expanded view of the infinite possibilities of choice. There is no longer any separation between our animal, human, and divine selves.

Remember that you have the ability to choose your actions and reactions in each moment. Becoming the Cosmos card does not imply perfection or never making another mistake. It means embodying all of you with great love and awareness, and choosing with awareness over and over until all of your choices are based in an openhearted love. We are reborn beyond our limitations of our ego and into a universe where everything is possible.

When you have a DEFICIENCY of Cosmos energy, you probably
- Are self-absorbed
- Have a narrow view of the world

When you have an EXCESS of Cosmos energy, you probably
- Have no sense of self
- Focus exclusively on the suffering of the world

SYMBOLS to help you dream the Cosmos card:

WREATHS
The dancer is surrounded by a wreath with twenty-two elements, which represents the final integration of major arcana. The figure also wears a wreath on its head, denoting victory.

INFINITY
The infinity symbols of the Magician and Strength cards tie the top and bottom of the wreath together, showing union beyond duality in Earth and Sky.

SPIRALS
The central figure holds two spiral wands that act as antennas to Spirit. One spirals clockwise and gathers energy while the other spirals counterclockwise and sends energy.

VEIL

The central veil is in the shape of the Hebrew letter Kaph, the symbol for hand. The hand of Spirit gently holds us, so we become a channel for divine grace. Kaph is the Hebrew letter for the Wheel of Fortune. Having integrated the Wheel's lessons, we are now beyond it.

FIGURES IN CORNERS

Another echo of the Wheel of Fortune card, the four figures now act as guardian Angels. Notice how the Bull (a representation of the Fool) has turned toward the infinite.

HEBREW LETTER: TAV / MARK

This letter is a sign of finality, agreement, joyful completion, and the ultimate end of a cycle.

COSMOS COLORING INSTRUCTIONS

White: Clouds (edged in violet), bull's horns.
Yellow: Eyes of eagle and lion, eagle's beak.
Blue: Sky.
Green: Wreath (except for infinity signs), leaves on head wreath.
Red: Flowers on wreath, infinity signs.
Violet: Veil of Kaph around dancer.
Brown: Animals, lion is more tawny (a little yellow added).
Silver and Gold: Stars in the sky, left spiral silver, right spiral gold.

Acknowledgments

Dedicated to Raven Smith for his encouragement, sweet love, and early morning giggles.

Many blessings to RMaya, Anya Grossman, and Jai Cross for their editorial wisdom and polishing prowess. Jai, you are truly my Hanuman.

Gratitude to all SpiritWeavers — past, present, and future. May you shine brightly.

And heartfelt thanks to the magnificent Jump! Circle of Diana Adkins, Jai Cross, Quinn Fitzpatrick, Dave Hendrix, Rainbow Marifrog, Trisha McWaters, Cindy McPherson, Billie Lee Mommer, and Shine Staub — You continue to amaze and inspire me. Bingo!

– Heather Ash

I want to dedicate my gratitude to all the ways the pitfalls and challenges have inspired the realization of these pages. A heartfelt thanks to my dear friends and teachers Heather Amara and Raven Smith for the opportunity to shine and work with me in the most fierce and loving ways to create the "portals" of magic that oozed from my imagination and fingertips, and yes, sometimes had to be dragged out as they kicked and clawed their way into being. Mom, Ultan and Storm: you are the creators of my creation!

There are so many beautiful people to thank and dedicate these images to for so many reasons, so I'll simply dedicate it to all beings everywhere — that you may laugh, love, and learn as I have through the entire birthing process of these images.

The DIVINE resides within these "portals" and I truly wish that all who gaze at them see and feel that sacred reflection always and ever.

-- Indigo

Bibliography

Ash, Heather. *The Four Elements of Change.* Council Oak Books, 2004

Jayanti, Amber. *Living the Qabalistic Tarot.* Weiser Books, 2004.

Greer, Mary. *Tarot for Yourself.* New Page Books, 2002.

Nelson, Mary Caroll. *Beyond Fear.* Council Oak Books, 1997.

Noble, Vicki. *MotherPeace* Harper San Francisco, 1994.

Noble, Vicki and Jonathan Tenney. *The MotherPeace Playbook.* Wingbow Press, 1986

Ruiz, Miguel. *The Four Agreements.* Amber-Allen Publishing, 1997.

Ruiz, Miguel. *The Mastery of Love.* Amber-Allen Publishing, 1999.

Sharman-Burke, Juliet. *Mastering the Tarot.* St. Martin's Griffin, 2000.

Wanless, James. *Voyager Tarot.* Merrill-West Publishing, 1986.

Toltec Center Offerings

Books

The Four Elements of Change by Heather Ash $15
Want to know how to stop your disaster mind? Or how to clear out old, stagnant emotions? Or to truly nourish yourself from the inside out? Heather Ash offers powerful guidance and insights into how to heal and balance your mental, emotional, energetic, and physical being..

The Recapitulation Workbook by Raven Smith $15
Recapitulation is one of the most effective tools we have found for creating lasting transformation. Learn how to reclaim energy you have lost in the past so you can use it to fuel your desired future. This step-by-step workbook gives clear instruction and practices to unlock your full potential.

Stop Seeking, Start Being! by Heather Ash Amara and Raven Smith $15 Integrity is a return to wholeness, a weaving together of our fragments into a solid core. What would it be like to live in your integrity in all aspects of your life, and be deeply, unshakably connected to Spirit?

Audio

Returning to Center: Meditation and Recapitulation by Heather Ash $15 Our bestselling audio CD. At the request of her students, Heather Ash created this CD to ground you in your center each morning, and then gather back any energy you lost during the day. This CD will teach you how to be more present, centered, and effective with your precious time.

The Four Elements of Change CD by Heather Ash $15 Connect with guides from each of the elements (air, fire, water, and earth) during this CD's magical visualization. Then learn specific tools, some of which are not included in the book, for embodying each element: increasing your awareness, energy, and self-love. Music by Indigo Flores.

Living an Impeccable Life by Heather Ash, $15 What would it be like to be impeccable each moment of your day? What is the difference between impeccable and trying to be perfect? Learn how to get out of the perfect trap and step into your authenitic integrity.

Shamanic Tools, a five-CD set $55 This packed series was recorded live in Hawaii. It blends the best of the Four Elements and the Four Agreements. A great introduction to the clarity, humor, and joy of Heather Ash.

Visit our bookstore at http://www.tolteccenter.org

For additional practices and guidance on the Tarot,
visit our website at: http://www.toltectarot.com

Calendar of events and additional free articles,
are available at:
http://www.tolteccenter.org

//// Toltec Center Resources

Teotihuacán, Mexico

Toltec Tarot Journeys

Join Heather Ash Amara and Raven Smith for an unforgettable journey to the heart of Toltec wisdom, Teotitihuacan. This ancient initiation ceremony is a joyous celebration of the beauty and fullness of life, and an incredible way to release old agreeements and limitations. Take your life to the next level!

TESTIMONIALS

"My trip to Teotihuacan was more than transformational, it was heart-opening beyond my wildest imaginings. Heather Ash and Raven are not only superb teachers, they also provide a tender container of safety for growth and expansion." TM, Texas

"This group of strangers became my sacred family. I was gently lead through the most life-transforming experience. My life will never be the same." CW, Tennessee

"Coming to Teotihuacan is a gift to your soul. It is an acknowledgement that the deepest yearnings of your being can and will be manifest in your life." RM, California

FOR UPCOMING DATES
Visit http://www.tolteccenter.org

Free Newsletter

Sign up for our monthly newsletter at
http://www.tolteccenter.org

Toltec Tarot Tunes

Our very own Lesley Lishman was so inspired by the writing and poetry in this book that she created a song for each tarot card. From the Fool through the World, her songs encapsulate the playful wisdom of each unique tarot archetype! You can find it in the store at
http://www.tolteccenter.org

Made in United States
Troutdale, OR
10/11/2023